CHILDREN'S PARTY CAKES

CHILDREN'S PARTY CAKES

Maxine Clark ♦ *Joanna Farrow* ♦ *Kathy Man*

Macdonald Orbis

A *Macdonald Orbis* BOOK

© Macdonald & Co (Publishers) Ltd 1988

First published in Great Britain in 1988
by Macdonald & Co (Publishers) Ltd
London and Sydney

A Pergamon Press plc company

British Library Cataloguing in Publication Data
Clark, Maxine
   Children's party cakes.
   1. Cake decorating—Amateur's manuals
   I. Title   II. Farrow, Joanna   III. Man,
   Kathy
   641.8'653   TX771

ISBN 0-356-15522-6

Filmset by SX Composing Limited, Rayleigh, Essex
Printed and bound in Italy by New Interlitho

Senior Commissioning Editor: Joanna Lorenz
Art Director: Bobbie Colgate-Stone
Designer: Frances de Rees
Photographer: Vernon Morgan
Stylist: Sue Russell
Illustrator: Mary Tomlin

Macdonald & Co (Publishers) Ltd
Greater London House
Hampstead Road
London NW1 7QX

CONTENTS

Basic Recipes, Equipment & Techniques

F *antasy cake making relies not only on decorating techniques and artistic effort but on successful baking in the first place. The basic cakes need to be moist, tasty and firm, not only for eating but for cutting and shaping. Recipes for different sponge cakes and a fruit cake follow, although of course if you have your own favourite recipes these can be used instead. It is important to use the exact quantities of given ingredients when following cake recipes, but you should also remember that stated oven temperatures and cooking times may vary slightly according to your own oven's temperament – make any minor adjustments as necessary.*

Recipes and step-by-step methods for making the various icings and fillings are in the following pages, including fondant, royal and gelatine icing, marzipan, glaze, frosting and buttercream. However, mail-order suppliers and stores are listed at the back of the book for certain icings and decorating materials if you cannot face making your own.

Next, a checklist of cake baking and decorating equipment is described, and there is an invaluable section on the different baking and decorating techniques used in this book. Step-by-step instructions show you how to grease and line all shapes of cake tin, and how to cover the baked cakes with marzipan and different types of icing. The book then shows how to colour icing and marzipan with food colouring, and piping techniques are explained with the help of illustration. Finally, there are tips for making and using templates, and on how to make icing and chocolate run-outs for special designs.

The main section of the book follows with the thirty spectacular cake recipes, each with a colour photograph and helpful step-by-step colour illustrations to make the recipes easy to follow. There are cross-references to the basic recipes at the beginning of the book where appropriate.

Basic Recipes

QUICK SPONGE CAKE

This cake mixture is perfect for the children's cakes in this book, as it is light and moist yet firm enough to handle and cut into different shapes. It is extremely simple to make as everything is mixed together all at once, with no special beating or whisking involved.

Quick sponge cake is best made the day before using (or earlier), as the cake will then be much easier and less messy to cut and shape. The cake can be kept for two to three days in the refrigerator and can also be frozen while still uniced.

Because this cake mixture uses baking powder to make it rise rather than gradual incorporation of air while beating, make sure you do not overbeat the mixture or add more than the specified amount of baking powder – this would only serve to toughen the cake and make it heavy.

Basic cake quantity

225g (8oz) soft margarine
225g (8oz) caster sugar
5 eggs (size 3)
300g (10oz) self-raising flour
5ml (1tsp) baking powder
15ml (1tbsp) milk

Method

1 First preheat the oven to 170°C (325°F/Gas Mark 3) and grease and line the required cake tin – in the case of this basic quantity, a 20 or 23cm (8 or 9inch) round tin or an 18 or 20cm (7 or 8inch) square tin. See page 17 for details on preparing cake tins.

2 Place all the ingredients in a large bowl and beat well with a wooden spoon for 1–2 minutes until the mixture is smooth. (Alternatively, blend in an electric mixer.) Turn into the prepared cake tin and smooth the top level.

3 Bake the cake for the time specified in the chart, or in the case of the basic quantity given here, about 1 hour. Leave to cool slightly in the tin before turning out and transferring to a wire rack to cool completely.
See baking chart on page 8.

VICTORIA SPONGE CAKE

Although this is not so good as the quick sponge or madeira cake for cutting and shaping, it is ideal for the simpler shaped fantasy cakes and its advantage over the quick sponge is that it is lighter. It does not keep so well, so make and ice the cake shortly before it is to be eaten.

This cake can be flavoured in an endless variety of ways to suit personal tastes – a few are listed in the chart on page 9, but add your own ingredients as liked. For instance, coffee sponge can be made by adding a tablespoon of coffee (first dissolved in a little hot water), or add 1 tablespoon lemon juice for a moist lemony cake.

Basic cake quantity

175g (6oz) butter or margarine, softened
175g (6oz) caster sugar
3 eggs (size 3)
175g (6oz) self-raising flour, sifted

Method

1 First preheat the oven to 180°C (350°F/Gas Mark 4), and grease and line the required tins – in the case of this basic quantity, two sandwich or one deep 18 or 20cm (7 or 8inch) round tin(s) or two sandwich or one deep 15 or 18cm (6 or 7inch) square tin(s). See page 17 for details on preparing cake tins.

2 Place the butter or margarine in a bowl with the sugar, and cream together until light and fluffy using a wooden spoon. Gradually beat in the eggs, one at a time – if you add them too quickly the mixture may curdle. Add a little sifted flour if the mixture begins to separate.

3 Sift the flour over the mixture in the bowl and fold in quickly and gently with a metal spoon. Do not overbeat the mixture. Turn into the prepared cake tin(s) and smooth the surface level.

4 Bake the cake(s) for the time specified in the chart, or in the case of the basic quantity given here, about 25 minutes until golden and just firm when lightly pressed. Leave to cool slightly in the tin(s) before turning out and transferring to a wire rack to cool completely.
See baking chart on page 9.

Quick Sponge Cake Chart

The quantities below will fill one deep (7.5cm/3inch) cake tin of the size stated. The tins should be prepared beforehand (see page 17), and any pudding basins or mixing bowls used should be ovenproof. Follow the method on page 7.

CAKE TIN SIZES	12cm (5in) round	12cm (5in) square 15cm (6in) round 1.35ltr (2½pt) mixing bowl	15cm (6in) square 18cm (7in) round	18 or 20cm (7 or 8in) square 20 or 23cm (8 or 9in) round 1.85ltr (3¼pt) mixing bowl 900g (2lb) loaf	23cm (9in) square 25cm (10in) round 20×25×7.5cm (8×10×3in) rectangle
INGREDIENTS Soft butter or margarine	100g (4oz)	150g (5oz)	175g (6oz)	225g (8oz)	275g (9oz)
Caster sugar	100g (4oz)	150g (5oz)	175g (6oz)	225g (8oz)	275g (9oz)
Eggs (size 3)	2	3	3	5	6
Self-raising flour	150g (5oz)	200g (7oz)	225g (8oz)	300g (10oz)	325g (11oz)
Baking powder	2.5ml (½tsp)	2.5ml (½tsp)	5ml (1tsp)	5ml (1tsp)	10ml (2tsp)
Milk	10ml (2tsp)	10ml (2tsp)	15ml (1tbsp)	15ml (1tbsp)	30ml (2tbsp)
VARIATIONS **Chocolate:** substitute cocoa powder for same of flour	15g (½oz)	15g (½oz)	25g (1oz)	40g (1½oz)	50g (2oz)
Mint: add 1. mint essence	1.25ml (¼tsp)	2.5ml (½tsp)	5ml (1tsp)	7.5ml (1½tsp)	10ml (2tsp)
2. green food colouring	few drops	few drops	few drops	few drops	few drops
Citrus: add grated orange or lemon zest	1 small fruit	1 small fruit	1 large fruit	2 small fruit	2 large fruit
OVEN TEMPERATURE	170°C (325°F/ Gas Mark 3)	170°C (325°F/ Gas Mark 3)	170°C (325°F/ Gas Mark 3)	170°C (325°F/ Gas Mark 3)	170°C (325°F/ Gas Mark 3)
COOKING TIME (approx.)	35–40 minutes	50 minutes	55 minutes	1 hour	1 hour

Victoria Sponge Cake Chart

The quantities given below will fill either one deep (7.5cm/3inch) cake tin of the size stated, or two shallow sandwich tins. The tins should be prepared beforehand (see page 17), and any pudding basins or mixing bowls used should be ovenproof. Follow the method on page 7.

CAKE TIN SIZES	12cm (5in) square 12 or 15cm (5 or 6in) round	15 or 18cm (6 or 7in) square 18 or 20cm (7 or 8in) round	20cm (8in) square 23cm (9in) round	23cm (9in) square 25cm (10in) round 20×25×7.5cm (8×10×3in) rectangle	1.35ltr (2½pt) pudding basin	1.85ltr (3¼pt) mixing bowl
INGREDIENTS Soft butter or margarine	100g (4oz)	175g (6oz)	225g (8oz)	400g (14oz)	225g (8oz)	350g (12oz)
Caster sugar	100g (4oz)	175g (6oz)	225g (8oz)	400g (14oz)	225g (8oz)	350g (12oz)
Eggs (size 3)	2	3	4	7	4	6
Self-raising flour	100g (4oz)	175g (6oz)	225g (8oz)	400g (14oz)	225g (8oz)	350g (12oz)
VARIATIONS **Chocolate:** substitute cocoa powder for same of flour	15g (½oz)	25g (1oz)	40g (1½oz)	50g (2oz)	40g (1½oz)	50g (2oz)
Citrus: add grated orange or lemon zest	½ fruit	1 fruit	2 small fruit	2 large fruit	2 small fruit	2 large fruit
Cherry and almond: add 1. chopped glacé cherries	50g (2oz)	65g (2½oz)	65g (2½oz)	75g (3oz)	65g (2½oz)	75g (3oz)
2. almond essence	2.5ml (½tsp)	5ml (1tsp)	5ml (1tsp)	7.5ml (1½tsp)	5ml (1tsp)	7.5ml (1½tsp)
OVEN TEMPERATURE	170°C (325°F/ Gas Mark 3)	170°C (325°F/ Gas Mark 3)	170°C (325°F/ Gas Mark 3)	170°C (325°F/ Gas Mark 3)	170°C (325°F/ Gas Mark 3)	170°C (325°F/ Gas Mark 3)
COOKING TIME (approx.)	20 minutes	25 minutes	30 minutes	35–40 minutes	1–1¼ hours	1½ hours

RICH FRUIT CAKE

This wonderfully rich and moist fruit cake may be a little strong for many young children's tastes, but it is a lovely alternative for an older child, for a special occasion such as Christmas, or when the cake needs to be kept for some time. This cake mixture will improve the longer it is kept, and should be stored well wrapped in non-stick paper and a double thickness of foil. Keep in a cool, dry place.

Basic cake quantity

190g (6½oz) butter or margarine
190g (6½oz) soft dark brown sugar
3 eggs (size 3)
225g (8oz) plain flour
1.25ml (¼tsp) salt
7.5ml (1½tsp) ground mixed spice
450g (1lb) raisins and currants
225g (8oz) sultanas
65g (2½oz) glacé cherries
40g (1½oz) flaked almonds
3.75ml (¾tsp) grated citrus zest

Method

1 First preheat the oven to 140°C (275°F/Gas Mark 1), and grease and line the required cake tin – in the case of this basic quantity, a 20cm (8inch) round tin or an 18cm (7inch) square tin. See page 17 for preparing cake tins.

2 Cream the butter or margarine in a mixing bowl with the brown sugar until light and fluffy. Then beat in the eggs lightly, one at a time.

3 Sift the flour, salt and ground mixed spice together and then fold gradually into the creamed butter and sugar mixture.

4 Add all the remaining ingredients (the fruit and nuts) to the bowl, and stir well until mixed evenly. Do not beat the mixture. Turn into the prepared cake tin and smooth the top. Make a very slight dip in the centre of the cake as this will help it to rise more evenly.

5 Bake the cake for the time specified in the chart, or in the case of the basic quantity given here, about 3–3½ hours or until a skewer inserted into the centre comes out clean. Leave to cool in the tin before turning out. **See baking chart on opposite page.**

MADEIRA SPONGE CAKE

Madeira sponge is a good choice for many cakes as it is moist and tasty, yet firm and compact enough for cutting and shaping. It also has a lovely lemony flavour that is popular with children and adults.

The madeira cake is cooked at a fairly low oven temperature as overheating halts the action of the raising agent and the cake becomes rather solid. Uncooked madeira cake mixture can be frozen in an airtight container. To freeze cooked, wrap in cling film when cool.

Basic cake quantity

175g (6oz) butter or margarine
175g (6oz) caster sugar
3 eggs (size 3)
175g (6oz) self-raising flour
75g (3oz) plain flour
15ml (1tbsp) lemon juice
grated zest of 1 lemon

Method

1 First preheat the oven to 170°C (325°F/Gas Mark 3), and grease and line the required cake tin – in the case of this basic quantity, a 20cm (8inch) round tin or an 18cm (7inch) square tin. See page 17 for details on preparing cake tins.

2 Place the butter or margarine in a bowl with the sugar, and cream together until light and fluffy using a wooden spoon or, if liked, an electric whisk. Gradually beat in the eggs, one at a time, ensuring that each is thoroughly mixed before adding the next one.

3 Sift the flours together in another bowl and fold quickly and gently into the creamed mixture in three batches. Do not overbeat the mixture. Fold in the lemon juice and zest.

4 Pour into the prepared cake tin and smooth the top level. Bake for the time specified in the chart, or in the case of the basic quantity given here, about 1 hour and 10 minutes or until a skewer inserted into the centre comes out clean and dry.

5 Leave to cool in the tin for 15 minutes before turning out and transferring to a wire rack to cool completely. **See baking chart on page 12.**

Rich Fruit Cake Chart

The quantities below will fill one deep (7.5cm/3inch) cake tin of the size stated. The tins should be prepared beforehand (see page 17), and any pudding basins or mixing bowls used should be ovenproof. Follow the method opposite.

CAKE TIN SIZES	12cm (5in) round	12cm (5in) square 15cm (6in) round 1.1ltr (2pt) pudding basin or mixing bowl	15cm (6in) square 18cm (7in) round 900g (2lb) loaf	18cm (7in) square 20cm (8in) round 2ltr (4pt) pudding basin or mixing bowl 17×25×7.5cm (6½×10×3in) rectangle	20cm (8in) square 23cm (9in) round	23cm (9in) square 25cm (10in) round 20×25×7.5cm (8×10×3in) rectangle
INGREDIENTS Soft butter or margarine	90g (3½oz)	100g (4oz)	150g (5oz)	190g (6½oz)	275g (9oz)	375g (13oz)
Soft dark brown sugar	90g (3½oz)	100g (4oz)	150g (5oz)	190g (6½oz)	275g (9oz)	375g (13oz)
Eggs (size 3)	2	2	3	3	4	6
Plain flour	100g (4oz)	150g (5oz)	175g (6oz)	225g (8oz)	350g (12oz)	450g (1lb)
Salt	pinch	pinch	pinch	1.25ml (¼tsp)	2.5ml (½tsp)	2.5ml (½tsp)
Ground mixed spice	2.5ml (½tsp)	5ml (1tsp)	5ml (1tsp)	7.5ml (1½tsp)	10ml (2tsp)	15ml (1tbsp)
Raisins	100g (4oz)	150g (5oz)	225g (8oz)	300g (10oz)	450g (1lb)	575g (1¼lb)
Currants	75g (3oz)	100g (4oz)	150g (5oz)	175g (6oz)	225g (8oz)	350g (12oz)
Sultanas	75g (3oz)	100g (4oz)	175g (6oz)	225g (8oz)	350g (12oz)	450g (1lb)
Glacé cherries	40g (1½oz)	50g (2oz)	50g (2oz)	65g (2½oz)	75g (3oz)	150g (5oz)
Flaked almonds	15g (½oz)	25g (1oz)	25g (1oz)	40g (1½oz)	50g (2oz)	75g (3oz)
Grated citrus zest	1.25ml (¼tsp)	2.5ml (½tsp)	2.5ml (½tsp)	3.75ml (¾tsp)	5ml (1tsp)	7.5ml (1½tsp)
OVEN TEMPERATURE	140°C (275°F/ Gas Mark 1)	140°C (275°F/ Gas Mark 1)	140°C (275°F/ Gas Mark 1)	140°C (275°F/ Gas Mark 1)	140°C (275°F/ Gas Mark 1)	140°C (275°F/ Gas Mark 1)
COOKING TIME (approx.)	1½ hours	1½–2 hours	2 hours	3–3½ hours	3½–4 hours	4–4½ hours

Madeira Sponge Cake Chart

The quantities below will fill one deep (7.5cm/3inch) cake tin of the size stated. The tins should be prepared beforehand (see page 17), and any pudding basins or mixing bowls used should be ovenproof. Follow the method on page 10.

CAKE TIN SIZES	12cm (5in) square 15cm (6in) round	15cm (6in) square 18cm (7in) round	18cm (7in) square 20cm (8in) round 1.1ltr (2pt) pudding basin 16.5×27×7.5cm (6½×10½×3in) rectangle	20cm (8in) square 23cm (9in) round 2ltr (4pt) pudding basin	23cm (9in) square 25cm (10in) round 24×30×7.5cm (9½×12×3in) rectangle	25cm (10in) square 27.5cm (11in) round
INGREDIENTS Soft butter or margarine	75g (3oz)	100g (4oz)	175g (6oz)	225g (8oz)	300g (10oz)	350g (12oz)
Caster sugar	75g (3oz)	100g (4oz)	175g (6oz)	225g (8oz)	300g (10oz)	350g (12oz)
Eggs (size 3)	2	2	3	4	5	6
Self-raising flour	75g (3oz)	100g (4oz)	175g (6oz)	225g (8oz)	300g (10oz)	350g (12oz)
Plain flour	40g (1½oz)	50g (2oz)	75g (3oz)	100g (4oz)	150g (5oz)	175g (6oz)
Lemon juice	10ml (2tsp)	10ml (2tsp)	15ml (1tbsp)	20ml (4tsp)	25ml (5tsp)	30ml (2tbsp)
Grated lemon zest	½ fruit	½ fruit	1 fruit	1½ fruit	2 fruit	2½ fruit
OVEN TEMPERATURE	170°C (325°F/ Gas Mark 3)	170°C (325°F/ Gas Mark 3)	170°C (325°F/ Gas Mark 3)	170°C (325°F/ Gas Mark 3)	170°C (325°F/ Gas Mark 3)	170°C (325°F/ Gas Mark 3)
COOKING TIME (approx.)	50 minutes	1 hour	1 hour 10 minutes	1 hour 20 minutes	1½ hours	1 hour 40 minutes

Fondant Icing Chart

QUANTITY OF FONDANT REQUIRED (Refers to amount of icing sugar used)	350g (12oz)	450g (1lb)	675g (1½lb)	900g (2lb)	1.5kg (3lb)	2kg (4lb)
INGREDIENTS Liquid glucose	15ml (1tbsp)	50g (2oz)	75g (3oz)	100g (4oz)	175g (6oz)	225g (8oz)
Egg white	1 small	1 large	2 small	2 large	3 large	4 large
Icing sugar	350g (12oz)	450g (1lb)	675g (1½lb)	900g (2lb)	1.5kg (3lb)	2kg (4lb)

FONDANT ICING

Sometimes called moulding icing, fondant is used in the majority of recipes in this book. It is easy to mould and form into any shape, and is used in large sheets for covering cakes as well as for making edible decorations and objects. Fondant is easily coloured (see page 21 for instructions on how to mix with food colouring), and although soft and pliable it will harden sufficiently for painting and forming into free-standing objects. The advantage of fondant over royal icing for covering cakes is that it is much easier and quicker to make, is more pliable and has a softer texture that many people prefer.

The recipe given here is a quick-to-make fondant that does not need cooking. One basic quantity (450g/1lb) is sufficient to cover a 20–23cm (8–9inch) round cake. Fondant is also available ready-made in many specialist stores and can be obtained by mail-order. See page 118 for details and addresses. Keep unused icing wrapped tightly in aluminium foil or cling film. It will remain soft for about 24 hours if kept in this way. Roll out and mould fondant using a little icing sugar or (preferably) cornflour for dusting to help prevent sticking.

Basic quantity

50g (2oz) liquid glucose

1 large egg white (size 2)

450g (1lb) icing sugar, sifted

Method

1 Place the liquid glucose and egg white in a large mixing bowl. Gradually mix in the sifted icing sugar, beating well to a thick smooth paste.

2 As the mixture becomes too stiff to stir, turn it out on to a surface dusted with cornflour or icing sugar and knead in the remaining icing sugar. Knead well until completely smooth and very firm. If the fondant feels a little dry, add a few drops of water and knead in well.

3 Colour as desired and keep wrapped in cling film or aluminium foil until ready to use, to prevent it from drying out.

See baking chart on page 12.

ROYAL ICING

Royal icing is used when a harder icing is needed, for covering cakes, securing items and for delicate piping work. Although more difficult to make than quick fondant icing, the technique is soon mastered. Royal icing takes a little practice to spread evenly and pipe, but the results are well worth the effort.

Although royal icing should be firm, it should not be so hard that it cannot be cut with a knife. Made from a mixture of egg white and icing sugar, it involves vigorous beating to incorporate as much air as possible. The amount of icing sugar needed cannot be exact, as it depends upon the consistency of icing required for the use you have in mind. Icing for covering cakes can be quite stiff, although a little liquid glucose (about 1 teaspoon to 450g/1lb icing sugar) could be added for some softness. To harden a royal icing, for instance where it is used as part of a structure or decoration, a tiny amount only of acetic acid or cream of tartar could be added. To whiten and add elasticity to icing for piping purposes, a squeeze of lemon juice is used.

When making royal icing, ensure that your equipment is clean and completely grease-free, as even the slightest trace of egg yolk or oil will prevent the mixture from becoming properly aerated. It is also better to beat the icing in a china, glass or metal bowl rather than plastic which can leave tiny particles in the mixture. Keep the icing covered with a damp cloth at all times, as it quickly develops a crust. Royal icing can be stored, wrapped tightly, in the refrigerator for up to two days.

Adjust the quantities for the amount required using the same quantities of icing sugar and egg white. A 2 egg/450g (1lb) quantity is enough to cover a small cake in one layer, and a 1 egg/225g (8oz) quantity is sufficient for piping and 'glueing' purposes.

Basic quantity

1 egg white (size 3)

225g (8oz) icing sugar, sifted

Method

1 Place the egg white in a mixing bowl and beat until frothy. Gradually add the icing sugar, a little at a time, beating well with each addition until the mixture holds its shape.

2 Place a piece of cling film directly on top of the icing and another piece of cling film over the top of the bowl to prevent the icing from drying.

MARZIPAN

Marzipan is used not only for adding interest and flavour to a cake but as an 'undercoat' for cake coverings and also for modelling. It is particularly important for covering fruit cakes and cakes with an uneven surface, as it provides a smooth area for the icing and prevents discoloration of the icing by the cake if it is going to be kept for some time.

The recipe here is for a simple marzipan that needs no cooking. Home-made marzipan has a better flavour than most shop-bought varieties, and is much paler in colour – particularly important when food colourings are added. However, you can substitute shop-bought marzipan or almond paste if desired – some addresses of mail-order suppliers are listed on page 118.

Marzipan can be used as soon as it is made, but keep unused quantities well wrapped in aluminium foil or cling film in a cool place, preferably the refrigerator. Ideally, it should not be kept for more than two to three days before using. Marzipan can also be frozen for up to six months.

This basic quantity makes 450g (1lb) of marzipan, which is just sufficient to cover a 23cm (9inch) round cake. If you are using the marzipan to cover a cake (see page 19 for details of this), remember that the cake will then need to be left to dry out thoroughly before covering with icing.

QUANTITY OF MARZIPAN REQUIRED	450g (1lb)	675g (1½lb)	900g (2lb)
INGREDIENTS Ground almonds	225g (8oz)	350g (12oz)	450g (1lb)
Caster sugar	100g (4oz)	175g (6oz)	225g (8oz)
Icing sugar	100g (4oz)	175g (6oz)	225g (8oz)
Egg	1	1 large or 2 small	2
Almond or vanilla essence, or lemon juice	2.5ml (½tsp)	3.75ml (¾tsp)	5ml (1tsp)

Basic quantity

225g (8oz) ground almonds

100g (4oz) caster sugar

100g (4oz) icing sugar

2 eggs (size 3)

2.5ml (½tsp) almond or vanilla essence, or lemon juice if preferred

Method

1 Place the almonds and both the sugars in a mixing bowl and mix well together.

2 Beat the eggs well with the essence or juice, and stir into the sugar mixture. Mix to a stiff paste, using your hands if necessary. Do not overwork the mixture, however.

3 Wrap the marzipan in cling film or polythene to prevent drying out and keep in a cool place until needed.

AMERICAN FROSTING

American frosting is a meringue-like soft icing alternative for covering sponge cakes, and is used especially for its fluffy effect and whiteness. This particular recipe is a quick-to-make version, and is ready to use in about ten minutes. Use immediately after making.

An electric hand or rotary beater can be used to whisk the icing mixture. Flavourings can be added to the mixture before whisking if desired, such as a little mint essence or citrus zest and juice.

Basic quantity

175g (6oz) caster sugar

1 large egg white (size 2)

pinch of salt

pinch of cream of tartar

Method

1 Place all the ingredients in a mixing bowl and stand the bowl over a saucepan half full of gently simmering water. Whisk the mixture continuously until it thickens and stands in peaks. Do not let the bowl become too hot however, or the mixture will cook before it can thicken.

2 Use the frosting straight away to cover the sponge cake, making decorative swirls with a small palette knife.

BUTTERCREAM

Buttercream is a popular filling and occasional topping for sponge cakes, and is used in many of the fantasy cakes in this book. Cakes filled with buttercream will keep if kept in an airtight container for up to two weeks, but it does go off quicker than other types of icing. Unused buttercream will freeze well until needed.

Various flavourings can be added to the mixture to suit personal tastes. Add a little vanilla essence for vanilla buttercream (about 1.25ml/¼tsp per 75g/3oz icing sugar), or perhaps orange or lemon juice for a citrus cream (add 5ml/1tsp per 75g/3oz). To make chocolate buttercream, add 15g (½oz) cocoa powder to the mixture, and for a coffee flavour add 5ml (1tsp) coffee – either first dissolved in a little water or the 'Camp' variety. Beat the flavouring into the finished buttercream until well blended.

Basic quantity

100g (4oz) butter or margarine, softened
225g (8oz) icing sugar, sifted
10ml (2tsp) boiling water

Method

1 Place the butter or margarine in a mixing bowl and beat well until light and fluffy. An electric whisk can be used if liked.

2 Gradually beat in the sifted icing sugar, adding a little at a time and mixing until well incorporated. Add the water and beat until the mixture is light and fluffy.

QUANTITY OF BUTTERCREAM REQUIRED (Refers to amount of icing sugar used)	75g (3oz)	175g (6oz)	225g (8oz)	350g (12oz)	450g (1lb)
INGREDIENTS					
Butter or margarine	40g (1½oz)	75g (3oz)	100g (4oz)	175g (6oz)	225g (8oz)
Icing sugar	75g (3oz)	175g (6oz)	225g (8oz)	350g (12oz)	450g (1lb)
Boiling water	2.5ml (½tsp)	5ml (1tsp)	10ml (2tsp)	15ml (1tbsp)	20ml (4tsp)

GELATINE ICING

Gelatine icing is useful for some decoration as it sets quickly and quite hard. It is mainly used for modelling, but can also be used for covering cakes.

Gelatine icing can, if liked, be used instead of fondant icing in recipes. It needs to be used as soon as it is made, however, as it quickly becomes too tough to handle and shape. Keep all unused icing tightly wrapped in cling film while you work.

Basic quantity

10ml (2tsp) gelatine
450g (1lb) icing sugar, sifted
1 large egg white (size 2)
10ml (2tsp) liquid glucose

Method

1 Mix the gelatine in a small mixing bowl with 30ml (2tbsp) of hot water. Stand the bowl over a saucepan of gently simmering water and stir until dissolved.

2 Place the icing sugar, egg white and liquid glucose in another, larger, mixing bowl and mix together. Quickly beat in the gelatine to form a smooth dough and knead well in the bowl.

3 Colour as required and wrap in cling film or in a polythene bag to prevent drying out. Leave for 1 hour, then knead again before using.

APRICOT GLAZE

Apricot glaze is used for securing icing and marzipan to basic cakes, and is useful as a barrier to prevent cake crumbs from being mixed up with the icing. It is extremely simple to make – just warmed jam with a little water. If liked, 1 teaspoon of rum could be added for extra flavour.

Basic quantity and method

Press 30ml (2tbsp) jam through a sieve into a small saucepan. Add 15ml (1tbsp) water and cook over a gentle heat until the jam has melted. Brush the glaze while still hot over a fruit cake, but allow to cool slightly before spreading over a sponge cake.

Basic Equipment & Techniques

The correct equipment is particularly important for cake making and decorating and can make your work much easier. The equipment used in this book is not specialist or complicated, but a thorough checklist is given here of the many items available. All equipment should be clean and dry before using.

CAKE TINS

A wide variety of cake tins are used in this book, of many shapes and sizes. Ovenproof pudding basins and mixing bowls are also used for interesting cake shapes – the basin gives a sharply domed cake and the bowl a wider, more gently sloping line. Some recipes in the book require other containers such as empty food cans for a tubular effect. The following cake tins are used in the recipes:

round deep tins – 12cm (5in) ranging up to 27.5cm (11in)
round shallow (sandwich) tins – 12cm (5in) ranging up to 27.5cm (11in)
square deep tins – 15cm (6in) ranging up to 25cm (10in)
square shallow (sandwich) tins – 15cm (6in) ranging up to 25cm (10in)
loaf tin – 900g (2lb)
swiss roll tin – 23×30cm (9×12in)
rectangular tins – 17×25×7.5cm (6½×10×3in)
         – 20×25×7.5cm (8×10×3in)
         – 24×30×7.5cm (9½×12×3in)
pudding basins – 1.1ltr (2pt)
         – 1.35ltr (2½pt)
         – 2ltr (4pt)
mixing bowls – 1.35ltr (2½pt)
         – 1.85ltr (3¼pt)

For preparing and lining the different shaped tins, see the detailed instructions on pages 17–18.

CAKE BOARDS AND DRUMS

These are available in many sizes and shapes, even hexagonals and hearts. They are usually covered with silver or gold paper, and can be found in most department stores and kitchen accessory shops.

Cake drums are the thicker of the two, being about 1cm (½inch) thick. They are most commonly used in this book. Cake boards or cards could be made at home from thick card and foil.

Cake drums are generally re-usable – just scrape off all the icing gently with a plastic spatula and wipe clean with a damp cloth.

TURNTABLE

This item is not absolutely necessary, but is very helpful for moving the cake around easily while you are involved in delicate icing work. It also creates a lovely spinning effect for presenting cakes – the roundabout and carousel cakes (see page 97 and 63) would look very special on a turntable.

ROLLING PIN/SMOOTHERS

These are essential for rolling out and smoothing icing and marzipan. A wide, wooden heavy rolling pin is best. (Make sure too that you have a large, smooth surface for rolling out.) Smoothers or 'spacers' can be plastic or metal, and even come with handles. They are used to create a perfect finish on iced cakes, and often have a decorative edge that can be used to imprint patterns on the icing. Use a flexible plastic smoother for fondant icing, and a small stainless steel scraper for royal icing.

MIXING BOWLS

An obvious requirement – it is best to use glass or china bowls only, however, to avoid possible discoloration of the icing.

SPATULAS/PALETTE KNIVES

A selection of small and large metal spatulas or palette knives is very useful for spreading icing on top and around the edges of cakes. Palette knives can also be used for 'peaking' icing to create a grass- or sea-like effect.

CUTTERS

Pastry and biscuit cutters are useful for cutting different shapes out of cake and fondant icing. Made from stainless steel, cutters are also available in tiny ('aspic') sizes and in numerals.

PAPER/FOIL/CLING FILM

All these are essential for most baking and cake decorating procedures. Use a good non-stick or greaseproof paper such as bakewell or parchment for lining cake tins, and as a base for moulding and piping icing. Waxed paper and aluminium foil are also used.

Cling film or polythene bags are required for keeping unused icing tightly wrapped and air-free at all times, as otherwise it quickly dries out.

PIPING BAGS AND NOZZLES

Absolutely necessary for most of the fantasy cakes in this book, and for all cake decorating. Complete icing sets can be bought from many kitchenware and department stores, and usually consist of a piping bag and six of the most commonly used nozzles. Nylon is the best material for piping bags as it wears well and is easy to wash. For some icing work, it is possible to make a small disposable bag out of a cone of non-stick paper, snipping off the very tip for a tiny nozzle (see page 22 for details).

A wide range of nozzles is used in this book. Made from plastic or metal, the nozzles are inserted straight into the bag or, to save emptying the piping bag unnecessarily, attached on to a screw adaptor. The most commonly used nozzles in the recipes in this book are a fine writing (No.1), a medium writing (No.2), a small star (No.5), a larger star (No.11 or 12), and a basket-weave (No.22 or 48). Generally, the smaller the number the finer the nozzle – the No.1 nozzle is used for lettering. See page 23 for more details on nozzles and piping techniques.

PAINT BRUSHES

A selection of fine-tipped artist brushes is invaluable for painting icing and marzipan with food colouring, and can be used for delicate detailing such as facial features or modelled figures and other objects, and for large-scale washed effects.

MODELLING TOOLS

Although most moulding and shaping can be achieved with your fingers and the help of utensils such as knives and cocktail sticks, a set of professional modelling tools is a good idea if you plan to make a lot of fantasy cakes. They come in a variety of shapes and sizes, including shell and blade shapes, paddle and 'U' shapes, cones and stars, and balls and bones.

COCKTAIL STICKS/SKEWERS

Wooden cocktail sticks and skewers are used in a few of the cakes in this book for propping up, for securing and also for decorative items such as flagpoles. They are also very useful for marking delicate lines on to marzipan and icing, and for precise work where fingers would be too large and clumsy.

OTHER KITCHEN EQUIPMENT

Other useful items that are standard kitchen equipment include a wire cooling rack, a selection of whisks and wooden spoons, a good range of sharp knives, a plastic or metal sieve, and a flour shaker for dusting surfaces with icing sugar or cornflour to prevent sticking.

OTHER USEFUL ITEMS

Plasticine is useful to have at hand for propping up items of icing and marzipan while they are drying. You may also need various items such as pencils, an icing ruler (invaluable for measuring dimensions and trimming in straight lines), a pair of scissors and some string.

PREPARING CAKE TINS

To bake a cake with an even, smooth finish, correct lining and greasing is important. The lining paper used should be non-stick, whether greaseproof, parchment, baking paper, bakewell or brown. The paper needs to be packed well into the tin for a smooth edge, and is best used double thickness for greater insulation and easy removal.

Use the following techniques for lining tins for quick and madeira sponge cakes, and for fruit cakes. You do not need to line tins for Victoria sponge cake as it is so light, but a circle or square of paper cut to fit the bottom of the tin will ensure an easy turn-out. Otherwise, lightly grease the tin and then dust with flour and caster sugar.

Lining a round tin

1 Place the cake tin base down on a sheet of paper (double thickness if necessary), and draw round it with a pencil. Cut out the circle just inside the marked line (to allow for the thickness of the tin) so that you have a round.

2 To line the sides of the cake tin you need to cut a strip of paper (or two, for double thickness), as long as the circumference of the tin – allowing a little for overlap – and about 1cm (½inch) wider than its depth. Fold up one side of the strip's length to a depth of 1cm (½inch) and make snips along the length up to this folded line. The snips should be at intervals of 5mm (¼inch).

3 Press the strip around the inside of the tin so that the snipped edge tucks neatly around the base, overlapping to allow the paper to curve. Press the round(s) of paper into the base of the tin. Lightly grease the entire surface of the paper base and sides.

Lining a square or loaf tin

1   Place the cake tin on the paper (double thickness if required), base down, and draw around the edges with a pencil. Cut out the square or rectangle just inside the marked line to allow for the thickness of the tin.

2   To line the sides of the cake tin, cut a strip as long as the combined edges of the tin (allowing a little for overlap) and about 1cm (½inch) wider than the cake tin's depth. It is easiest to measure the length of the strip by placing the tin on the paper and turning it over four times – mark each corner of the tin on the paper with a pencil, for folding.

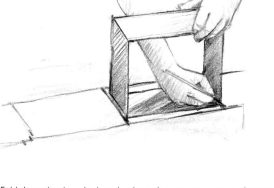

3   Fold the strip along its length where the corners occur so that you have a sharp, straight crease for each angle of the tin. Unwrap the strip. Then, fold up the length of the strip to a depth of 1cm (½inch) and make snips up to this folded mark at the points where the large corner creases occur – four or five in all.

4   Press the strip around the inside of the tin so that it fits neatly into the square or loaf tin. The bottom fold will overlap at the corners so that the paper fits in snugly. Make sure that the paper is pressed well into the corners. Press the base paper into the tin and grease the entire inside of the tin lightly and evenly.

Lining a rectangular or swiss roll tin

1   Place the cake tin on the paper (double thickness if required), base down, and mark around it with a pencil. Cut out the rectangle, 5cm (2inches) larger than the pencil mark all the way round to allow for overlap. Then, snip diagonally into each corner of the paper rectangle, to a depth of 5cm (2inches).

2   Press the paper into the tin – the snipped corners will overlap so that the paper fits snugly into the tin. There will be a slight overlap over the top of the tin. Brush the paper lightly with grease.

Lining a pudding basin or mixing bowl

1   Brush the edges of the basin well with grease. Line the bottom of the basin only with paper by cutting out a circle of paper about 5cm (2inches) larger than the base of the bowl. Make cuts into this paper circle to a depth of 5cm (2inches) all the way round.

2   Press the paper circle into the base of the bowl so that the snips overlap up the sides and the round fits the base snugly. Grease the paper lightly.

Lining an empty food can

1   Remove the paper wrapping from the can and carefully remove the top and base with a can opener. Wash and dry the can well, and place upright on a greased baking tray.

2   To line the can, cut out a rectangle of paper as long as the circumference of the can and as wide as its depth. Allow 1cm (½inch) on each side for overlap, and wrap the paper inside the can. Grease well.

3   To line the base, place the can on a piece of paper and draw round it. Cut out a circle, 1cm (½inch) outside the line, and cut snips into the circle all the way round to a depth of 1cm (½inch). Grease and press the base down into the tin so that the snipped pieces fold up around the sides of the tin.

COVERING CAKES

Covering with marzipan

Covering a cake with marzipan gives a smooth, even base for icing as well as added flavour interest. It also prevents discoloration of icing by the cake if it is to be kept for a while. Marzipan is not essential for many of the cakes in this book, but is a nice addition if you have the time.

Marzipan can be bought or home-made (see page 14). Allow the cake to cool thoroughly before applying the marzipan.

1 Dust your working surface with icing sugar or cornflour to prevent sticking and place the cake upside down on the surface. This is so that the flatter base becomes the top, ensuring a smoother surface to the cake. If there are any holes or dips in the cake, these can be filled in now with a little marzipan and glaze. Trim the edges of the cake if they are uneven.

2 Take half the marzipan and roll out to an area that is the size of the cake to be covered – square, circular or rectangular depending on its shape. If liked, you can transfer the marzipan to a sheet of non-stick paper now to make inverting it with the cake easier.

3 Brush the smooth top of the cake with apricot glaze (see page 15) and turn it over on to the centre of the marzipan, glaze side down. Press down firmly. Trim away excess marzipan from around the edge of the cake with a knife and carefully turn the cake, with the marzipan topping, the right way up.

4 To cover the sides of the cake, roll out a long strip of marzipan as long as the circumference of the cake and as wide as its depth (hint: the circumference of a round cake is three times its diameter). For a round cake, the strip can be one continuous piece; for a square or rectangle, cut a strip for each side.

5 Brush the edges of the cake with apricot glaze and press the strip along the sides. For a round cake, roll the cake like a wheel along the strip, picking up and pressing on the marzipan as you go. For a square or rectangle, just press each side on to the cake.

6. Smooth the corners neatly and trim away any excess. Smooth the whole cake carefully with the heels of your hands to give a perfect finish.

Alternatively, the marzipan could be simply rolled out into a large area and transferred to the cake in one piece. Drape over, press down over the top and sides, and smooth to fit over the corners before trimming away excess around the base. This method gives a more rounded surface, suitable for fondant icing but not for a more formal royal-iced cake.

Covering with fondant icing

Fondant icing is the most popular form of cake covering used in this book. It is particularly suited to fantasy cakes as it is easy to use and provides a soft, smooth surface. It can even be applied without an undercoat of marzipan. Dust working surfaces with a little icing sugar or cornflour when rolling out, to prevent sticking.

1   Roll out the fondant icing into a large round or square (depending on the size and shape of the cake to be covered), about 10cm (4inches) larger all round to allow for the sides.

2   Brush the top sides of the cake surface with glaze, or, if already covered with marzipan, with a little boiled water. (If liked, a little rum or brandy could be added to the water as a sterilizing agent.) If the cake has not been covered with marzipan, make sure that you invert the cake so that the smooth under-side becomes the flat top surface of the finished cake.

3   Dusting your hands with icing sugar or cornflour to prevent sticking, care-fully pick up the fondant by sliding your hands underneath it. Transfer to the cake and drape over. Smooth the fondant over the top and down the sides of the cake, making sure that the corners are smooth and defined.

4   Trim away excess icing from around the base with a knife. To give a smooth polish to the fondant, a plastic icing smoother can be pressed over the surface of the cake.

Covering with royal icing

This is quite difficult to apply, and is used more for fancy and wedding cakes than for fantasy cakes such as those described in this book. However, if a hard smooth surface is required royal icing is very effec-tive. It is also used in many of the cakes for decorative effects, piping, and backgrounds that are peaked up with a palette knife so that the icing hardens into a choppy surface to represent grass or sea.

1   Place some of the royal icing on the top of the marzipan-covered cake and spread over with a palette knife, taking care to press out any air bubbles. Using a straight edge such as a ruler or edge of an icing smoother, scrape the top of the cake in even sweeps, in one direction only.

2   Spread the remaining icing round the sides and, using a spatula or icing smoother, scrape flat and even. Make sure that the top edge of the cake is even

and neat. A turntable is invaluable when icing the sides of a round cake, as one hand can turn the cake while the other gently applies the smoother in one continuous movement.

3   Leave to harden for about 24 hours before, if a very professional finish is required, applying a second and then a third thin coat.

COLOURING AND PAINTING

There are many different kinds of edible food colourings on the market, available in felt tip form, pastes, dry powders, syrups and liquids. The range of colours available is large, and a list of mail-order suppliers is given on page 118 if your local grocer or store does not stock them. Do check the labels first, although most brands now provide food colourings that are non-toxic and harmless. However, gold and silver colourings, though stunning in effect, do not taste pleasant and it is suggested that they are not eaten in any quantity.

The liquids and pastes generally give the strongest effects. Liquid colours are best used for painting and tinting, and where colours need to be paler. Paste colour provides a rich intense shade without thinning down the fondant and marzipan as with liquids. Lustre powder is included as an optional ingredient in some of the cake recipes in this book – a non-toxic shiny coloured powder, this can be brushed on to dry icing to give a lovely shimmering effect.

Colouring

Take the amount of marzipan or fondant that needs to be coloured and form into a ball. Dip a cocktail stick into the food colouring and transfer to the ball, streaking the colour over the top. (The cocktail stick is used to ensure that only the amount of colour needed is applied – it is easy to overdo it. For large quantities of fondant or marzipan, the tip of a teaspoon could be used.) Do not make holes to press colour into the ball, as air pockets may result.

Knead the fondant or marzipan thoroughly, using a circular motion to spread the colour evenly. If a darker shade is required, knead more colour in. To see if the colour has been distributed evenly, cut a slice off the ball and check inside.

Some of the recipes require a marbled effect. In this case, just knead the colour in slightly so that it is unevenly distributed before rolling out – a marbled pattern will result.

To shade royal icing, colouring is best added at the end of mixing.

Note: Remember that many food colourings take a little while to develop to their full intensity after being added to icing or marzipan, especially in the case of red and black.

Painting

Painting food colour directly on to icing and marzipan instead of kneading it in has a number of advantages. It means that greater detail is possible, for instance on little figures and for decorative patterns. The intensity of the colour achieved is also much greater, as the shades become of necessity slightly diluted when mixed into icing. Subtle wash effects can be used to great effect on iced backgrounds, where different coloured fondants would be too strong. For colouring large areas or items of icing or marzipan, however, it is still better to shade the icing first so that a more even tone is obtained – painting over a large area in a single colour can be patchy and uneven.

1   Use the food colouring as you would paint, using fine paint brushes and a white saucer for a palette. Use the colourings straight from the tube or bottle, or diluted for a paler shade. Colours can of course be mixed together for an infinite variety of results.

2   To blend colours on icing, as for instance on a sky background, apply the colours with a paint brush and then, while they are still wet, brush lightly across where they meet so that they merge subtly into each other.

3   If you wish to paint one colour directly next to another, it is best to let the first dry thoroughly before applying the second. To apply paint over another, for instance detail over a washed background or 'filling' for an outline, again allow the paint to dry completely first.

4   Certain special effects can be achieved easily with food colouring. For wood graining (as used in the treasure chest on page 106), simply apply winding brush strokes along a brown washed background in a slightly darker brown, splaying the brush tip out slightly to create a blurred variegated line. Paint with varying amounts of pressure for a realistic appearance.

PIPING TECHNIQUES

Piping bags and nozzles are used in virtually every recipe in this book. The techniques involved are quite simple, although it is a good idea to practise first with spare icing if you are unused to handling icing and piping bags. Remember too that the consistency of the icing to be piped will affect the handling – for instance buttercream is much runnier (and perhaps easier) to manage than thick royal icing.

The piping or icing bags need to be washed and dried with every change of colour icing, although of course if you have a number of bags available this is unnecessary, and a variety of colours can be kept on hand at any one time. Another alternative is to use disposable paper bags – these are also much more flexible to work with and are good for very delicate piping. The method for making your own paper bags is described below, or you can buy packs of ready-to-assemble paper triangles from kitchenware stores and icing equipment suppliers.

To make a paper piping bag
1   Take a piece of non-stick paper, preferably waxed, and cut out a 25cm (10inch) square. Fold this in half diagonally to make a triangle. Pinching the centre of the long folded edge with one hand, bend the side corners of the triangle round into the centre so that all the corners meet together, to form a long pointed cone.

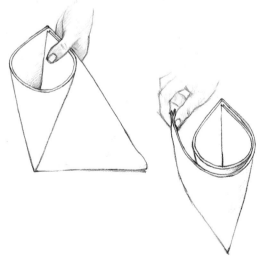

2   Fold in the overlapping corners at the top tightly, to secure the cone – you could staple it down as well if you like. The bag is then ready for filling: snip off the tip of the cone to the size of hole required. (It is better to cut a very tiny tip at first, test it out with icing on a piece of paper and then enlarge the hole if need be.) A nozzle can then be inserted into the bag if required.

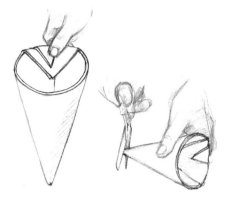

Filling the piping bag
Insert the required nozzle, if using, into the bag and spoon in the icing so that the bag is no more than two-thirds full. Push the icing down well into the bag, fold over the two corners into the centre and then the top corner over this. Fold over quite tightly so that the icing is well packed down.

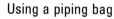

Using a piping bag
To hold a large piping bag, grip it so that your fingers are curled over the front of the bag and the folded corner twisted between your thumb and index finger. Press the icing out evenly by squeezing with your hand. (As the icing goes down, keep twisting to tighten the folded ends between your thumb and index finger.) Use your other hand to balance the bag as you work, if liked.

If using a tiny paper bag, you can just hold it between your middle and index finger and push the top down with your thumb. For very tiny pieces of piping, you could even put a little icing directly into the nozzle and press out with your thumb – messy but simple.

Piping straight lines

To pipe a straight line, hold the bag at a slight angle and press the nozzle on the surface. Squeeze out the icing smoothly, and raise the nozzle so that the icing comes out slightly suspended – it is then easier to drop exactly into place as you go. Do not drag the nozzle along the cake as the line will be ragged and uneven. Move your hand slowly and smoothly along the required line and stop squeezing a little before you reach the end of the line (because the flow continues after the pressure ceases). Drop the nozzle back on the surface to break off the icing and pull away neatly.

Nozzles: No.0.5 (very fine), No.1 (fine), No.2 (medium), No.3 (thick).

Piping stars or rosettes

To pipe stars, hold the bag at right angles to the surface to be iced, with the nozzle just a hair's breadth away. Press gently to squeeze out a star of icing, stop the pressure, and pull away the nozzle tip so that the icing star forms to a point and breaks off. If piping a solid row of stars, pipe a row of alternate stars first, allow to dry and then fill in the gaps with a second row of stars.

Nozzles: No.5 (very small), No.7 (small), No.9 (medium), No.11 (large), No.12 (very large). Alternatives are: No.15 (very large with more points), No.13 (very large with more points and finer ridged effect), and rope nozzles No.s 42, 43 and 44 (small ridged stars). No.s 27 and 31 also make attractive small stars.

Piping shells

These are made with the star nozzles, but are slightly elongated when piped. Hold the bag at right angles to the surface to be iced, with the nozzle a fraction away. Squeeze out a star, pull the bag slightly sideways to pull the star into a tail, and break off.

Nozzles: star nozzles, e.g. No.5 (very small), No.7 or 8 (small), No.11 (large), No.13 (very large).

Piping ropes

To create a twisted rope effect, pipe in a straight line but twist the bag as you are piping, keeping an even pressure on the icing all the time. Thick, ribbed or thin ropes can be made depending on the nozzle chosen. For very simple stranded ropes, use a plain writing nozzle.

Nozzles: No.42 (very small), No.43 (small), No.44 (medium), No.52 (very large).

Piping basket-weave

For this you will need both a plain writing nozzle and a basket-weave nozzle. First pipe vertical straight lines over the required area, evenly spaced apart (use the writing nozzle for this). Then, using the basket-weave nozzle, pipe horizontal bands across the vertical lines. Pipe the bands down one row at a time, leaving even gaps in between. Then pipe across the next vertical line so that the bands half-alternate with the former bands in a criss-cross fashion all the way down. Repeat over all the area to be covered.

Nozzles: plain writing (No.1 or 2) and basket-weave (No.22 or 48).

MAKING AND USING TEMPLATES

Templates are not essential for the recipes in this book, but are a useful way of transferring more complicated designs and outlines from paper to icing or cake. They can be used to trace the outlines and details of objects or shapes from books, for transferring your own free-hand designs, and for geometric shapes that need to be repeated exactly on the cake or icing. Whether you use templates because you are not sure of yourself artistically or just to make the piping and cutting easier on the cake, the technique involved is soon mastered. An example of a cake recipe that uses templates is the pop-up birthday card on page 66.

1   Draw or trace the required outline on to non-stick paper. For specific shapes such as a rectangle or semi-circle, where the shape is cut out to the exact dimensions required, card could be used. Cut out the shape if appropriate – there is no need to do this for fiddly outlines.

2   Place the template on the surface of the cake or sheet of icing. If it is traced on paper, transfer the outline to the cake or icing in one of two ways. One method is to draw over the outline again on the underside of the paper with a soft pencil, then turn the paper the right way up and place on the icing. Press over the outline once more so that the shadowy imprint of the pencilled lines will be transferred from the base of the paper to the icing. Alternatively, you could place the template on the cake and stick little pins in along the outline and any details. Remove the pins and paper to reveal a pricked outline on the icing. An outline of icing can then be piped over to cover the pin marks.

3   For a simple cut-out outline or geometric shape such as a circle, rectangle or wedge, just hold the cut-out on top of the icing with one hand while you lightly score around it with a pin using the other hand.

MAKING RUN-OUTS

Running-out is the technique used for creating a smooth, solid area of icing with an exact outline – not easy to achieve by straight-forward piping or cutting out from set icing. An outline is first piped directly on to the cake or on to non-stick (preferably waxed) paper. The shape is then filled in or 'flooded' with royal icing.

The royal icing used for run-outs or flooding needs to be very slightly runnier in consistency than usual, so mix in a little unbeaten egg white or water, a drop at a time, until you achieve a cream-like consistency.

Pipe on to paper, if you need to allow the design to dry before being transferred to the cake, or directly on to the cake if this is applicable, for instance if the run-out is to lie flat. For examples of using run-outs, see the speed cruiser cake recipe on page 73 (the lifebelts are made by this method).

1   First pencil the outline, if necessary, on to the waxed paper or cake. Then fit a piping bag with a writing nozzle (No.1 or No.2) and fill with royal icing of normal consistency.

2   Carefully pipe over the outline in a continuous line and allow to dry.

3   Fill a paper piping bag with royal icing that has been thinned slightly. A paper bag is best as you do not need a nozzle for flooding, and a hole can be snipped into the base of the paper cone at the last minute. Alternatively, a spoon can be used.

4   Squeeze or spoon the icing inside the outline, starting in the centre and gradually taking the icing out to the piped edging line.

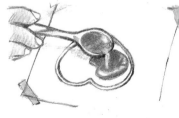

5 Use a cocktail stick if necessary to push the icing into awkward areas or corners. Do not touch the outline or it may break open, and avoid air bubbles forming, as these will spoil the smooth, sheer surface of the icing – if they do occur, prick with a cocktail stick.

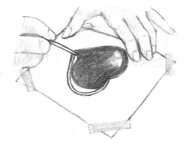

6 Leave the icing to set completely. If it is on paper, allow to dry for at least 48 hours before carefully peeling off the paper and transferring the run-out to the cake. Secure in place with little spots of soft royal icing.

Decoration run-outs

A similar technique is used when piping complicated or repeated designs such as lace patterns. Trace the outlines on to greaseproof or tracing paper, and fix a piece of waxed paper on top of this, securing firmly at the edges – this double layer is so that pencil marks do not attach themselves to the icing and discolour it. Pipe on to the waxed paper over the outlines, using a small No.0.5 or No.1 nozzle for very delicate work. Leave to dry overnight before gently bending back the waxed paper and lifting off the piped outlines with a palette knife. Attach to the cake surface as required.

Chocolate run-outs

Where certain shapes are required in chocolate, the run-out (or more accurately 'cut-out') technique is used. Melt the chocolate gently in a double sauce-pan or bowl set over a pan half full of gently simmering water – do not allow the chocolate to get too hot or it will separate. Blood heat should be the highest temperature for a smooth glossy result, although it takes more time to melt. Pour the chocolate out on to a sheet of waxed paper and tilt the paper in every direction to allow the chocolate to spread out evenly. Once set, the chocolate can be cut carefully into the required shape with a sharp non-serrated knife. Chocolate run-outs are used, for example, for the rabbit hutch roof and hinges on page 54.

The Cakes

Thirty spectacular cake recipes follow for a range of party cakes that will appeal to children of all age groups and tastes. Some cakes will be particularly attractive to younger children – for instance the colourful clown, the sheep with its woolly coat made from fluffy frosting, or the large tortoise nibbling a piece of lettuce. Older children might prefer the pirate's treasure chest brimming over with stolen loot, or the sophisticated speed cruiser and space rocket. Choose a cake with particular relevance to the child in mind, for instance a pet-owner or animal lover would be thrilled to receive an iced rabbit in a hutch, the frog sitting on its own water lily pond or the ponies in their stable. Children with a taste for the purely fairytale will love the magic fairy castle in the clouds, the snowy gingerbread cottage from Hansel & Gretel, or the fiery green dragon.

The details of the cakes can of course be adapted to suit your own inclinations, ability and time available. You may wish to stick to simpler objects and decorations than those described in the recipes, or to use different colours. If you are artistic, it may be fun to make any little figures in the shape and clothing of children at the party – for instance in the school bus cake, on the spinning roundabout or sliding down the helter-skelter. The name and age of the party boy or girl could be piped or painted on many of the cakes – perhaps across the large band of the hot-air balloon, on the space rocket or on the pop-up birthday card. Feel free to use the cakes here as a source of inspiration as well as a practical guide.

Every cake has a large full-colour photograph and helpful step-by-step illustrations to make the various recipe stages even clearer. There are cross-references to the basic recipes at the beginning of the book for the cake bases (whether sponge or fruit). Simply look up the cake tin size in the charts on pages 8–12 for all the ingredients, quantities and cooking times. Of course, if you prefer you can substitute a ready-bought cake of the same size, or a cake made to your own favourite recipe. Fondant icing, royal icing and marzipan can either be made using the recipes at the beginning of the book or purchased ready-made (see page 118 for a useful list of stores and mail-order suppliers).

Woolly Sheep

This cheeky sheep is easy to make, being based around a swiss roll cake. It is a relatively small cake, and so you might like to make a 'flock' of two or more if there are lots of children to feed. It would also be good for an Easter tea table.

Ingredients

2 eggs (size 2)

50g (2oz) caster sugar

40g (1½oz) plain flour

2 tablespoons cocoa powder

pinch of baking powder

225g (8oz) chocolate buttercream (p.15)

50g (2oz) desiccated coconut

100g (4oz) royal icing (p.13)

4 chocolate flakes

175g (6oz) fondant icing or marzipan (p.13 or 14)

175g (6oz) American frosting (p.14)

food colourings: green, black, yellow

icing sugar or cornflour for dusting

Materials and decoration

30cm (12inch) round cake drum

2–3 cocktail sticks or wooden skewers

brown paper

length of green ribbon

Equipment

23×30cm (9×12inch) swiss roll baking tin

non-stick paper

balloon whisk or hand beater

palette knife

piping bag with fine writing (No.1) nozzle

paint brush

Method

1 First make the swiss roll sponge. Line the 23×30cm (9×12inch) tin with non-stick paper. Place the eggs and sugar in a bowl placed over a pan of simmering water and whisk with a balloon whisk or electric hand mixer until very pale and thick. The whisk should leave a ribbon trail in the bowl when lifted out. Do not allow it to become too hot or the mixture will cook and not expand properly.

2 Remove from the heat and whisk until cool. Sift in the flour, cocoa and baking powder and then carefully fold together. Pour into the prepared tin, level carefully and bake in a preheated 180°C (350°F/Gas Mark 4) oven for 12–15 minutes. Have ready a sheet of sugared non-stick paper, remove the cake from the oven and turn out immediately on to the sugared paper. Peel off the lining paper and roll up with the sugared paper. Allow to become completely cold.

3 When cold unroll and remove the paper. Spread the sponge with the chocolate buttercream, covering all the sponge except for 1cm (½inch) at one short end. Roll the cake up towards that end and hold in place just for a few minutes.

4 Colour the desiccated coconut with green food colouring for grass. Spread a little royal icing, first coloured green, over the cake drum and sprinkle the coconut over.

5 Turn the cake so that the seam side is uppermost. Make four small holes for legs on this seamed side, place a flake in each hole and then turn the cake over – it should stand upright. Place in the centre of the cake drum.

6 Colour some of the fondant or marzipan (about three-quarters) black and use to mould a sheep's head, dusting your hands with icing sugar or cornflour. Colour a little more fondant or marzipan yellow and roll into two tapering sausages. Curl to form the sheep's horns. Press on to the head, smoothing on to secure. Insert cocktail sticks or wooden skewers into the back of the head and use to secure the head to the body so that the nose touches the ground as if grazing.

7 Spread the American frosting over the body of the sheep and swirl with a palette knife so that it looks like a woolly coat.

8 Place the royal icing in a piping bag and pipe two dots on to the head for eyes. Using a paint brush, paint two black dots on to the eyes. Cut out eyelashes from brown paper and attach them above the eyes with a little royal icing.

9 Using spare fondant or royal icing, coloured green and yellow as appropriate, mould or pipe daisies on to the grass and for the sheep's mouth. Wrap the ribbon around the cake drum, securing with a little glue or royal icing.

Space-age Robot

*T*his robot is shaped in white icing and painted afterwards – this makes the basic
shaping of the cake a quick and easy process. The robot can be painted in any
colours and patterns of your choice, or you can use the photograph as a guide.
The cake isn't large, and so is best for a small party of children unless you wish to
make another robot as his 'friend'.

Ingredients

900g (2lb) loaf rich fruit cake (p.11)
apricot glaze (p.15)
900g (2lb) fondant icing (p.13)
food colourings: colours of choice such as yellow, blue, red, black, silver
icing sugar or cornflour for dusting

Materials and decoration

25cm (10inch) round cake drum
black and white patterned paper
sticky tape or glue
candle and holder

Equipment

cocktail stick
paint brush

Note: *Allow an extra day or overnight preparation time for icing to set.*

Method

1 Cut off one sloping short end of the cake to form a secure standing base. Cut out the two top corners (about 2.5cm/1inch down and along) to distinguish the head. Brush the cake with apricot glaze.

2 Roll out half the fondant icing on a surface dusted with icing sugar or cornflour to a 15×35cm (6×14inch) rectangle and use to cover the sides of the body. Then roll out a long thin strip of icing, about 5×15cm (2×6inches), and use to wrap around and cover the 'head'. While the icing is still soft, mark on 'trousers' and the lines of a belt with the back of a knife. Use a cocktail stick to make holes in the belt.

3 Cover the cake drum with paper, wrapping tightly and securing underneath with sticky tape or glue. Stand the cake upright on the drum.

4 Shape two elongated semi-circles of fondant, large enough to cover the shoulders and to extend 1cm (½inch) over the edges of the cake. Secure on to the cake with a dampened paint brush.

5 To make the arms, roll several small balls of icing, each about the size of an olive, and flatten them to 5mm (¼inch) thickness. Cut each in half. Lightly dampen one piece with water and secure under the shoulder extension. Continue adding the pieces in the same way until the arms come half-way down the body. Curve the robot's left arm so that it is ready to support the candle.

6 Shape two small blocks of icing and secure to the ends of the arms for hands. Press the candle, in its holder, into the left hand. Roll out a thick sausage of icing, about 7.5cm (3inches) long, and cut in half. Press into position over the shoulder pads, one half along each one. Cut two little strips to decorate the front of the shoulder pads and press on. Roll out a small rectangle of icing and secure on the body front for the chest panel.

7 Using the tip of a cocktail stick, mark fingers on the hands. Mark the child's initials on to the panel, and surround with a decorative border. Shape a small 'key' from fondant and stick over the panel. Cut out small square features for the face, dampen and press on. For the hair, cut out a square area with a geometric 'fringe' and press over the head. If liked, cut out a spanner and leave to dry before painting silver.

8 Roll a large ball of icing for the hat and flatten to about 2cm (¾inch). Position the hat on the robot's head and make decorative markings with the back of a knife. Shape a brim of icing and secure on the front of the hat. Roll another ball of icing, flatten slightly, cut in half and position for the feet. Leave the cake to dry out overnight.

9 The next day, using food colourings and a fine paint brush, paint the robot in appropriate colours.

Frog on a Pond

*O*nly the frog takes time to mould and paint realistically – the rest of the 'pond' is very simple, being a basic round cake. To save effort you could substitute a bought marzipan frog if liked, or even a plastic toy one. This is quite an elegant cake on a theme popular with children – other pond life could be included if you wish, such as goldfish or tadpoles.

Ingredients

two 20cm (8inch) round sandwich chocolate-flavoured Victoria sponge cakes (p.9)

100g (4oz) chocolate buttercream (p.15)

900g (2lb) fondant icing (p.13)

food colourings: blue, green, yellow, brown, black

icing sugar or cornflour for dusting

Materials and decoration

23cm (9inch) round cake drum

3 cocktail sticks

non-stick paper or rice paper

length of blue ribbon

Equipment

aluminium foil or non-stick paper

cocktail stick

paint brush

Method

1 Place one sandwich cake on the cake drum and spread with the buttercream. Top with the second cake.

2 Colour half the fondant icing with blue food colouring and roll out on a surface dusted with icing sugar or cornflour. Use to cover the cake, smoothing around the sides and over the cake drum. Trim off excess icing around the base.

3 Keep half the remaining fondant in reserve (tightly wrapped) for the frog. Colour all but an egg-shaped piece of the remaining fondant green. Roll the green icing out on a surface dusted with icing sugar or cornflour and cut out several heart shapes in varying sizes (between 1cm/½inch and 2.5cm/1inch at their widest points.) Cut small slits into the pointed ends so that they resemble waterlily leaves. Curve the leaves up slightly around the edges and transfer to foil or non-stick paper to dry out.

4 Next cut out long slender leaves, about 5–7.5cm (2–3inches) long and 1cm (½inch) at their widest point. Bend some of the leaves over and also leave to harden on foil or non-stick paper.

5 Take the egg-shaped piece of icing and use to form the waterlily flowers and dragonfly bodies. To make the flowers, take tiny balls of the icing between your fingers and flatten into petals. Curve their ends up slightly and leave with the greenery to harden. For the dragonflies, mould small curved lengths and mark on segments with a cocktail stick. Leave to dry.

6 Make the frog with the reserved fondant. Take a piece of fondant, about the size of a large egg, and roll into a smooth ball. Place it on a piece of foil or non-stick paper and extend one end with your fingers to form a small head, pinching between your fingers to form the appropriate shape. Pinch a mouth and eyelids on to the head, and press tiny balls of icing into position for the eyes. To make the limbs, roll two thin sausages of fondant (about 2.5cm/1inch long) and cut into 'fingers' at one end with a knife. Dampen with water and secure to the front of the frog. For the back legs, roll two longer, slightly fatter sausages of icing and flatten the ends for feet. Mark lines for webbed feet with the back of a knife. Bend these legs in half and secure on to the frog behind the front limbs. Leave to dry before painting.

7 Place the waterlily leaves around the top of the pond cake, securing on with small pieces of fondant. To assemble the flowers, secure several white petals together and stick a tiny ball of yellow coloured fondant on top. Make several more flowers in the same way and attach on to the waterlily leaves. Secure the long bullrush leaves around the pond, sticking on with a little fondant.

8 To make the bullrushes, take the cocktail sticks and press into the leaves around the side of the pond cake. Mould small pieces of white icing over the ends of the sticks and allow them to dry before painting brown.

9 When the frog is dry, paint it appropriately, using diluted green, yellow, brown and black food colourings. Allow to dry before positioning the frog over a cluster of waterlilies.

10 To finish the dragonflies, paint the bodies with brown and green food colourings, including green heads and dark eyes. Cut out tiny wings from non-stick or rice paper – four for each dragonfly – and paint on delicate lines of blue and green. Secure the wings to the side of the bodies behind the heads, two on each side. Place on to the pond.

11 Finally, wrap the ribbon around the edge of the cake drum, securing it on with glue or a little icing.

Creatures from Outer Space

*T*his unidentified flying spaceship on a far-away planet is full of little details that children love – the green aliens can be as weird and wonderful as your imagination. The cake is based on shallow dome sponges, cleverly achieved by only part-filling pudding basins and a mixing bowl with cake mixture. Because the candles are displayed horizontally, light them for as brief a time as possible to avoid wax falling on the icing.

Ingredients

quantity for 20cm (8inch) round lemon-flavoured quick sponge cake (p.8)

apricot glaze (p.15)

900g (2lb) fondant icing (p.13)

6 little candy sticks

food colourings: blue, black, green, red, silver, yellow

icing sugar or cornflour for dusting

Materials and decoration

30cm (12inch) round cake drum

candles

few grains long-grain rice

length of blue or silver ribbon (optional)

Equipment

two 450ml (¾pint) ovenproof pudding basins

3.5ltr (6pint) ovenproof mixing bowl

non-stick paper

4cm (1½inch) plain round cutter

cocktail stick

paint brush

potato masher or grater

Note: *Allow an extra day or overnight preparation time to allow icing to set.*

Method

1 Grease and line all three basins with greased non-stick paper. Barely half-fill the two small basins with lemon cake mixture and place the remainder in the large bowl. Bake at 170°C (325°F/Gas Mark 3), allowing 40 minutes for the small basins and 50 minutes for the large bowl. Turn out on to a wire rack to cool.

2 Cut the risen surfaces off the small cakes. Then, using a 4cm (1½inch) cutter, cut a round out of one cake for the spaceship base. (The other small cake will form the spaceship.) Brush the surfaces of all the cakes with apricot glaze.

3 Colour a third of the fondant (just over 300g/10oz) with blue food colouring. Roll half of this out thinly on a surface dusted with icing sugar or cornflour into a curved strip that will cover half the outer edge of the cake drum (about 10×35cm/4×14inches). Dampen the edges of the drum and position on the strip. Cover the other side of the drum in the same way, using the remaining blue fondant. Trim off the excess with a knife.

4 Colour another third of the fondant grey (using a tiny amount of black food colouring), and roll out into a circle about 25cm (10inches) in diameter. Lay the icing over the domed side of the large cake and tuck the edges underneath.

5 Position the large cake in the centre of the cake drum. Using the rounded end of an object such as a rolling pin, beaker or measuring spoon, make craters over the surface of the cake: first dust the object with icing sugar or cornflour then press the object into the fondant. Using your fingers, draw up the icing around the object to give the 'crater' its rim. (Shaping around various objects of different sizes will give a more interesting effect.)

6 Colour a little more fondant, about the size of an egg, with green food colouring and reserve, tightly wrapped, for the space creatures. Colour a similarly sized piece red, roll out and use to cover the 4cm (1½inch) spaceship base. Trim away excess around the base. Secure the base to one side of the 'planet' using a dampened paint brush.

7 Use the trimmings of red icing to cover the flat underside of the remaining small cake, the 'spaceship'. Roll out a little of the remaining white fondant and use to cover the top and sides of the spaceship. Cut a long strip of fondant to wrap around the bottom edge of the ship. Then, while still soft, decorate the sides of the ship by gently pressing the base of a potato masher or grater into the icing to leave indentations. Using a sharp implement, press small holes into the icing around the top for candles.

8 Roll out a small rectangle of fondant about 4×2.5cm (1½×1inch). Mark on vertical lines with a knife and transfer to foil or non-stick paper to harden. (This will form the walkway.) Then, shape a small triangular door from fondant and secure to the spaceship. Cut out five tiny circles of white fondant (to go on top of the spaceship) and place on non-stick paper. Leave all to harden overnight.

9 Meanwhile, cut out small rounds of white icing in various sizes, and arrange on the blue icing for the distant planets.

10 Press the candy sticks into the underside of the spaceship, spaced evenly around. Place the spaceship carefully on to the red spaceship base, so that the candy tips rest on the cake.

11 Using a brush, paint the centre of the doorway and the very top circle of the spaceship black. Place the rectangular walkway beneath the door, securing with a little icing. Paint the walkway and the spaceship silver. Secure the tiny white circles on top of the spaceship, on the black area.

12 Using a very fine brush or tip of a cocktail stick, paint silver stars on to the blue background. Using black food colouring diluted with water, shade 'dark' areas on to the planet. Then, paint the cut-out planets red, yellow or other appropriate colours. Stick the candles into the holes on the spaceship.

13 To make the space creatures, shape small ovals from the green icing and position on the cake. Top each with a smaller green ball for the head. Roll very thin sausage lengths for the limbs and secure to the bodies, marking on toes and fingers with the tip of a cocktail stick. Use pieces of long-grain rice stuck with tiny balls of icing to make antenna, and paint facial features using black food colouring and a cocktail stick or fine brush.

14 Finally, if liked, wrap the ribbon around the edge of the cake drum and secure on with a little glue.

Hansel & Gretel Cottage

This gingerbread cottage is straight out of the fairy tale. Children will have great fun choosing which sweets to pick off the house first. Choose the brightest, prettiest sweets and biscuits you can find to decorate it – and for a special festive occasion, you could even cover the entire cake with gold and silver sweets only.

Ingredients

20×25×7.5cm (8×10×3inch) deep rectangular Victoria sponge cake (p.9)
apricot glaze (p.15)
675g (1½lb) marzipan (p.14)
675g (1½lb) gelatine icing (p.15)
450g (1lb) royal icing (p.13)
selection of small biscuits and sweets
food colourings: brown, pink
icing sugar or cornflour for dusting

Materials and decoration

30cm (12inch) round cake drum
aluminium foil
toothpicks (optional)
length of silver ribbon

Equipment

non-stick paper
piping bag with fine writing (No.1) nozzle

Note: *Allow at least 2 days extra preparation time for icing to set.*

Method

1 Level the top of the cake and cut it into three rectangles widthways, two 10×20cm (4×8inches) and the other 5×20cm (2×8inches). Brush the tops of the two large rectangles with apricot glaze and place one on top of the other. Place the smaller rectangle on top, in the centre. Press firmly together. Place on the cake drum.

2 Carefully carve a slanted roof shape into the top two cakes, sloping down evenly on either side. Brush all over with the remaining apricot glaze. Roll out the marzipan on a surface dusted with icing sugar or cornflour to a large rectangle and use to cover the entire cake, smoothing over the corners and keeping a 'sloping' effect on the roof. Trim away excess from around the base of the cake.

3 Roll out two-thirds of the gelatine icing (about 450g/1lb) to 5mm (¼inch) thickness and cut out two large rectangles for the roof. (Measure the dimensions of the cake roof to check that the gelatine icing rectangles are the same.) Also cut out four chimney-sized rectangles, two longer and with sloping ends. Leave to dry on non-stick paper, spaced well apart. At the same time, take the trimmings, colour them brown, roll them out and cut out a door shape. Leave it all to dry on non-stick paper overnight.

4 Meanwhile, colour the remaining gelatine icing pink, and roll out to about 5mm (¼inch) thickness. Cut out pieces to fit the sides and ends of the house – measure the dimensions of the cake to check that the gelatine icing rectangles are the same size. Use to cover the sides of the house, securing with a little water or royal icing.

5 The next day, cut out little pieces of 'glass' from aluminium foil for the windows. Secure on to the long sides of the house (two on each side) with a little royal icing. Cut out another small round window from foil and stick on the front (short) side of the house, at the top.

6 Use a little royal icing to cement the two pieces of roof on to the sloping sides of the house, propping up the eaves with toothpicks too if necessary. Cement the four chimney sides together and secure on to the roof. Allow to dry overnight.

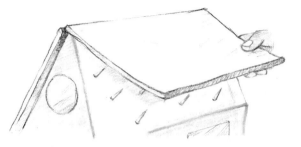

7 Using royal icing as cement, press the small biscuits and sweets all over the roof so that it is almost covered, and around the walls. Stick sweets into a door shape at the front of the house with royal icing.

8 Place some royal icing in a piping bag and pipe a handle and door knocker on to the sweet door. Pipe on window panes, and decorative borders around the windows, including a little 'frost' on the window panes if desired, and icicles on the overhanging eaves and on the chimney.

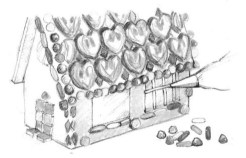

9 Spread the remaining royal icing all over the cake drum. Smooth a winding path towards the door, and spike up the 'snow' in the garden with the back of a teaspoon. Wrap the ribbon around the edge of the cake drum, securing with glue or a little royal icing. Add a garden path, flowers and any other suitable decorations as desired.

Big School Bus

*T*his bright red bus is large and suitable for serving quite a few children. To personalise it, the little figures in the bus could be made to look like the children at the party. If extra figures are needed, they could be placed sitting on the grass or even on the bus roof. The name of the birthday child is piped on to the bus number plate, with his or her age if liked.

Ingredients

four 16.5×27cm (6½×10½inch) rectangular madeira cakes (p.12)
500g (1lb2oz) buttercream (p.15)
apricot glaze (p.15)
900g (2lb) fondant icing (p.13)
450g (1lb) royal icing (p.13)
food colourings: red, black, pink, green, and other colours of choice
icing sugar or cornflour for dusting

Materials and decoration

35cm (14inch) square cake drum
length of red ribbon

Equipment

non-stick paper
paint brush
4cm (1½inch) plain round cutter
2.5cm (1inch) plain round cutter
piping bag with fine writing (No.1) nozzle and basket-weave (No.48) nozzle
palette knife

Note: *Allow an extra day or overnight preparation time for icing to set.*

Method

1 Cut 4cm (1½inches) off the ends of two of the rectangular cakes and sandwich all four cakes together with some of the buttercream, the shorter ones on top, centred widthways but aligned at one end. With a knife, carve a slope into the front of the two shorter cakes for the windscreen.

2 Carve out two small holes for windows along each side of the cake about halfway up. These should be about 4×5cm (1½×2inches) in area and 2.5cm (1inch) deep. Carve out a larger, shallower, window at the front for the driver, taking care not to weaken the cake too much or to make the edges too thin. Brush inside every window hole with apricot glaze.

3 Roll out white fondant (about 175g/6oz) on a surface dusted with icing sugar or cornflour, and cut out four squares about 10cm (4inches) to line the windows. (At the same time cut out two front side window shapes, and leave to dry out on non-stick paper until needed.) Neatly line all the hollowed-out windows with fondant, pressing in and trimming away excess at the edges. Cover the rest of the cake with the remaining buttercream.

4 Colour nearly half the remaining fondant (about 350g/12oz) red and roll out. Measure the height and width of each side of the bus – front, back, two sides and roof – and cut out pieces of non-stick paper to the same dimensions. Place these over the red icing and cut out the various sides. Cover the cake with the appropriate pieces of red fondant, smoothing into the angle on the front. Carefully locate all the window holes and neatly cut away the icing over them, smoothing over the joins.

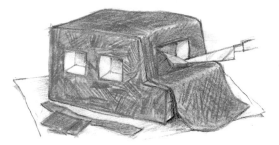

5 Roll out the red fondant trimmings and cut out thin (5mm/¼inch) strips for the window and door trimmings, and for trimming the edge of the roof. Secure on to the bus with royal icing.

6 Colour a quarter of the remaining fondant (about 75g/3oz) grey with a tiny amount of black food colouring and roll out to a 35cm (14inch) square. Cover the cake drum, smoothing on and trimming away excess around the base. Place the bus on the cake drum.

7 Using grey fondant trimmings, roll out and cut out long strips, 1cm (½inch) wide, to go around the base of the bus. Wrap around the bus and secure on with a dampened paint brush or a little royal icing.

8 Colour a little more fondant black (about 50g/2oz), roll out and cut out four 4cm (1½inch) circles with a cutter. Roll out the same amount of white fondant and cut out four more circles using a 2.5cm (1inch) round cutter. Fix the white discs on to the black discs to form wheels. Using black trimmings,

shape the front and rear bumpers and a rectangle for the radiator. Fix the bumpers and radiator, and then the wheels, on to the bus with royal icing.

9 With white fondant, cut out tiny circles for the front headlights and fix on. Cut out two thin rectangles for the number plates and leave to dry on non-stick paper before securing on. Fix the two side windows on to the bus with a little royal icing.

10 Use the remaining fondant icing to mould the children and the bus drivers. Colour some fondant fleshy pink for the faces and hands, and mould on to appropriately coloured torsos and arms. Make little fondant circles for hair, and press on. The steering wheel is made from a semi-circle of black or brown fondant. Leave the little figures and steering wheel to dry on non-stick paper for 24 hours. When dry, paint on facial features if liked, and insert into the windows, securing well with royal icing.

11 Put a little white royal icing in a piping bag with a writing nozzle and pipe thin lines down the front of the black radiator panel for the grille. You could also pipe stripes on to the children's clothing if liked. Then, using a basket-weave nozzle, pipe white lines down the middle of the grey road.

12 Colour a little more royal icing black and place in the piping bag with a writing nozzle. Pipe dots around the hubs of the wheels, the words SCHOOL BUS on to the front and back, and the name of the child and/or their age on to the front and back bumpers.

13 Use any remaining fondant and royal icing to make pavements and grass for the sides of the 'road'. Mould a very little black food colouring into some spare fondant to create a light marbled grey effect, and roll out a long strip to place along each side of the road. For the grass, colour royal icing green and spread on to the cake drum, making little tufts with a palette knife. Finally, wrap the ribbon around the edge of the cake drum, securing on with a little glue or royal icing.

Bag of Sweets

This simple but stylish cake – perfect for an older child or teenager – is easy to assemble, being a basic loaf cake. The sponge is flavoured with mint essence, but this could be omitted if preferred. The little sweets are made out of flavoured fondant and wrapped in cellophane, but bought wrapped sweets could be substituted as a short-cut if necessary.

Ingredients

900g (2lb) loaf mint-flavoured quick sponge cake (p.8)
apricot glaze (p.15)
900g (2lb) fondant icing (p.13)
2.5ml (½tsp) peppermint essence
food colourings: black, pink, green
icing sugar or cornflour for dusting

Materials and decoration

20cm (8inch) square cake drum
cellophane wrapping
length of pink ribbon

Equipment

2cm (¾inch) plain round cutter (optional)
aluminium foil or non-stick paper
paint brush

Note: *Allow an extra day or overnight preparation time for icing to set.*

Method

1. Using a knife, cut the sloping ends off both short sides of the cake. Turn the cake on to its long side and brush all over with the apricot glaze.

2. Take about 225g (8oz) of the fondant icing (about a quarter) and roll to a thick sausage on a surface dusted with icing sugar or cornflour. Dot with black food colouring. Fold the sausage in half then re-roll and fold two or three more times until the icing is streaked with the colour.

3 Dampen the cake drum with water. Roll out the coloured icing to a 20cm (8inch) square, very thinly to give a marbled effect. Transfer to the cake drum, press on and trim the edges. Position the cake on its side on the drum. (The risen surface of the cake should form the front.)

4 Reserve about 225g (8oz) of the remaining icing for the sweets, keeping tightly wrapped. Roll out a little of the remaining icing to a 7.5×15cm (3×6inch) rectangle and use to cover the top surface of the cake. Roll out more icing to two rectangles each about 11×18cm (4½×7inches), and use to cover the back and front of the cake. Roll out more icing (re-using any trimmings) into two 9×11cm (3½×4½inch) rectangles and use to cover the ends of the cake. Pinch the icing together where the edges meet.

5 Crumple up the edges slightly to resemble a paper bag. Using a knife dusted with cornflour, make 'bag' creases on the short sides of the cake. Make further decorative lines on the front and back of the cake with the back of a knife.

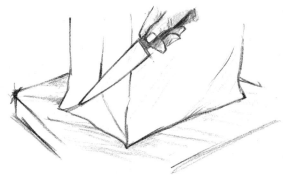

6 To make the sweets, knead peppermint essence into the reserved fondant. Colour one quarter pink, another quarter green and leave the remainder white.

7 Roll out the pink icing to 1cm (½inch) thickness and cut out small sweets about 2cm (¾inch) in diameter, using a knife or small cutter. Gather up the trimmings and roll out as thinly as possible. Roll out half the white icing to the same shape as the pink, and lightly dampen with water. Cover with the pink icing and roll up like a swiss roll. Cut into 5mm (¼inch) thick slices.

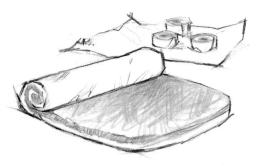

8 Use the green and remaining white icing to shape more sweets in the same way. Transfer the sweets to foil or non-stick paper and leave overnight to harden.

9 The next day, cut the cellophane into 9cm (3½inch) squares and use to wrap the sweets, twisting the ends.

10 Dilute a little green and pink food colouring with water and use to decorate the front of the bag with a fine paint brush. Leave to dry slightly then pile the sweets into the top of the bag and scatter the remainder around. Finally, wrap the ribbon around the cake drum and secure on with a little glue or royal icing.

Ballerina Doll

*T*his romantic Victorian ballerina is not as complicated to make as she looks. You could adapt the figure to make a fairy or a princess, just by adding paper wings or a crown. The ballerina here is cleverly perched on a matchbox so that she looks as if she is standing up, but you might find it easier to omit her feet and just stand her flat on the cake board.

Ingredients

1.35ltr (2½pint) pudding basin Victoria sponge cake (p.9)
apricot glaze (p.15)
225g (8oz) marzipan (p.14)
350g (12oz) fondant icing (p.13)
450g (1lb) royal icing (p.13)
silver lustre powder
sugar flowers
food colourings: pink, brown, silver, green
icing sugar or cornflour for dusting

Materials and decoration

15cm (6inch) round cake board
3 cocktail sticks
matchbox
cellophane
length of thin pink ribbon

Equipment

non-stick paper
piping bag with medium writing (No.2) nozzle, basket-weave (No.48) nozzle and star (No.27 or 31) nozzles
paint brush

Note: *Allow an extra day or overnight preparation time for icing to set.*

Method

1 Brush the cake with apricot glaze. Roll out the marzipan on a surface dusted with icing sugar or cornflour to a large circle and use to cover the cake, tucking the edges underneath and smoothing over the curve. Place on the cake board.

2 Colour the fondant icing a pink flesh colour. Use to model a head, a torso and two arms – mould the body and head together but the arms separately. Mould two small feet (with tapering calves) as well. Attach the arms to the torso with cocktail sticks. Leave all the limbs to dry overnight on non-stick paper.

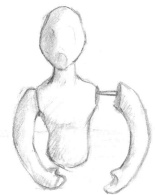

3 The next day, attach the body to the top of the cake with the help of a cocktail stick and a little royal icing. Prop the cake (with its board) on a low box such as a matchbox, to allow the skirt to drape down and the feet to point out underneath.

4 Colour a little royal icing brown and place in a piping bag with a medium writing nozzle. Pipe hair on to the ballerina and allow to dry.

6 Using the remaining royal icing and a small star tube, pipe little rosettes around the top of the body to form a heart-shaped neckline. Pipe a headdress around the top of the head. Leave to dry for a few hours. Meanwhile, pipe decorative lengths down the skirt at regular intervals, and little rosettes on top. Leave to dry.

5 Place some more royal icing (about 300g/10oz) in a piping bag with a basket-weave nozzle and pipe lines down from the waist to the hem. Do this all the way round the cake to form the frothy skirt, making sure that all the marzipan is covered.

7 Paint the top part of the ballet skirt – the body part under the neckline – a sparkly silver, using a paint brush and food lustre. Paint the decorative skirt rosettes silver, once the royal icing is dry. Paint a face and rosy cheeks on the ballerina's face with appropriate food colourings.

8 Gently secure the feet to the inside of the skirt with royal icing so that they point out. To make bouquets, stick sugar flowers on to long cones of green fondant with royal icing. Wrap little pieces of cellophane around and tie with lengths of thin pink ribbon.

Happy Whale Family

These plump and jolly whales – mother, children and baby – will be loved by all younger children. The little accessories and pieces of clothing can be adapted as you wish, and perhaps could be made relevant to the birthday boy or girl and guests. The tiny whales also make very good 'going home presents', although there will be arguments unless you make a few more. The spouting water sprays add a touch of authenticity, and are quite edible as they are made from rice paper.

Ingredients

24×30cm (9½×12inch) rectangular madeira cake (p.12)

350g (12oz) buttercream (p.15)

900g (2lb) fondant icing (p.13)

450g (1lb) royal icing (p.13)

food colourings; black, blue, green, and other colours of choice

icing sugar or cornflour for dusting

Materials and decoration

38cm (15inch) square cake drum

length of blue ribbon (optional)

rice paper

Equipment

non-stick paper

palette knife

paint brush

Note: *Allow an extra day or overnight preparation time for icing to set.*

Method

1 Trim the surface of the cake to give a completely flat surface. Divide the cake in half lengthwise so that there are two long strips of cake. Stack these one on top of the other and, holding the cakes steady with one hand, carve into a whale shape with a sharp knife. Carve a vertical curve on each side which tapers into one end, and a horizontal curve that tapers into the same end. Cut a thin slice of cake trimming to place on top of the head end to give extra height.

2 Cut four smaller whales from the cake trimmings, sticking pieces together as necessary with buttercream. Sandwich all the different parts of the large and small whales together with buttercream, and then spread all the remaining buttercream over the entire surfaces of the whales.

3 Colour three-quarters (about 675g/1½lb) of the fondant grey with a little black food colouring and roll out on a surface dusted with icing sugar or cornflour to a large area. Use to cover the whales, smoothing into the curves gently and tucking around the bodies. Make a small hole in the top of each whale for the spouts. Using grey fondant trimmings shape one large and four small whale tails, and mark on fin lines with the back of a knife or a cocktail stick. Leave the tails to dry on non-stick paper overnight.

4 Reserve a quarter of the royal icing (50g/2oz) and colour the rest in shades of blues and greens for the sea. Spread on to the cake drum, blending the colours together with a palette knife to create a sea effect. Make little peaks in the sea with the palette knife. If liked, wrap the ribbon around the edge of the cake drum, securing on with a little royal icing.

5 Secure the tails to the bodies of the whales with grey-tinted royal icing and smooth over the joints. The tails should tilt slightly upwards. Place the whales carefully on to the sea.

6 Cut out a rectangular strip of rice paper, about 10×20cm (4×8inches). This is to make the water spray for the large whale's 'spout'. Carefully snip into the paper along its length, to form a row of thin strands joined at one end. Roll up tightly into a tube, and insert into the whale spout, 'joined' end down. Use royal icing to glue the paper well into the spout. Gently bend the strips outwards to create the impression of water spray. Make the sprays for the small whales in the same way, cutting out four 6.5×10cm (2½×4inch) rectangles of rice paper.

7 Make eyes for the whales with little discs of white fondant topped with smaller discs of black, and fix on to the whales with royal icing or a dampened paint brush. Carve a smiling mouth line into each whale, and paint with a little black food colouring for definition.

8 Use the spare fondant to make accessories for the whales, if liked, colouring the icing in appropriate shades. To make a beach ball, mould two balls of different colours (such as red and blue) and slice each into even wedges. Take half the wedges from each to form a new ball, alternating the colours. To make a little nappy for a baby whale, cut out a triangle of white fondant and wrap around the base of the body before the tail is added, folding upwards and securing with a 'pin' – pipe on with royal icing and a medium writing nozzle and then paint with silver food colouring.

Rabbit Hutch

*T*his lovable white bunny in a hutch will endear itself to every child. If they have their own pet rabbit, make the bunny in an appropriate colour.
Although the cake and fondant icing can be prepared a week or so in advance if required, the chocolate work on this cake is best left until nearer the day.

Ingredients

23cm (9inch) square chocolate-flavoured quick sponge cake (p.8)

900g (2lb) fondant icing (p.13)

225g (8oz) royal icing (p.13)

apricot glaze (p.15)

200g (7oz) plain chocolate (a large bar)

food colourings: green, brown, blue, pink, orange

icing sugar or cornflour for dusting

Materials and decoration

30cm (12inch) square cake drum

length of brown ribbon

Equipment

lightweight saw or sturdy knife

aluminium foil or non-stick paper

piping bag with medium writing (No.2) nozzle

waxed paper

paint brush

Note: *Allow at least 2 days extra preparation time for icing to set.*

Method

1 Using a lightweight saw or sturdy knife, cut one end off the cake drum to make a 20×30cm (8×12inch) rectangle. Colour some fondant icing (about 225g/8oz) green and roll out on a surface dusted with icing sugar or cornflour to a similar-sized rectangle, and use to cover the cake drum, smoothing on and trimming the edges.

2 Reserve a quarter of the remaining fondant icing (keep tightly wrapped) and colour the remainder pale brown. Take some of the pale brown fondant – about 100g (4oz) – and roll out to a 9×10cm (3½×4inch) rectangle. Transfer carefully to a piece of foil or non-stick paper and cut out the centre of the rectangle to leave a thin frame of fondant. Carefully press on a tiny ball of brown fondant for the handle and leave to harden for at least 48 hours.

3 When the frame is dry, place the royal icing in a piping bag with a medium writing nozzle. Pipe horizontal and vertical lines evenly into the frame to form the latticed wired door. Leave to dry.

4 Cut the cake in half vertically. Sandwich the two halves together with glaze, one on top of the other, to form a large rectangle. Place in an upright position on the cake drum. Using a knife, cut a gently sloping slice off the top to resemble the roof of a hutch.

5 Roll out the remainder of the pale brown fondant and use to cover the sides of the cake. Mark wood panelling on the cake with the back of a knife, and mark a doorway on the left-hand side.

6 Break up the chocolate and place it in a bowl set over a saucepan of hot, but not boiling, water. Leave until melted. Turn the chocolate out on to a piece of waxed paper and lift the edges of the paper so that the chocolate spreads thinly over the surface. Leave until set.

7 Using a sharp knife, cut out a 12.5×23cm (5×9inch) rectangle for the roof from the chocolate. Also cut out two 'hinges' for the door of the hutch, and a 1cm (½inch) round for the handle. Using cool hands (wash under cold running water if necessary), transfer the roof to the cake and press down gently. Transfer the hinges and handle, securing with a little royal icing.

8 Make the rabbit. Take some of the remaining white fondant, roll to a ball and flatten to a 5cm (2inch) round. Press on to the front of the hutch for the rabbit's body. Mould a small ball for the head and secure it to the body with royal icing. Shape two long ears and a small bob-tail and position on.

9 From the remaining fondant and trimmings, shape several carrots and pieces of lettuce. Mould a little bird for the top of the hutch, if liked, from brown fondant trimmings. Using a paint brush paint blue eyes and whiskers on to the rabbit's face and pink ears and a nose. Colour the vegetable scraps green and orange, and paint the bird in appropriate colours. Paint wood markings on the hutch and its 'interior' behind the rabbit dark brown.

10 Carefully peel the paper off the hutch door. Pipe some icing down one short side of the hutch door and use to secure it to the hutch. Leave to dry out, supporting the door with jars until hardened into position. Place the vegetables around the hutch. Finally, wrap the ribbon around the edge of the cake drum, securing on with a little glue or royal icing.

Big Red Postbox

*T*his lovely old-fashioned British postbox sits in the middle of a village green. You can make any number of letters and parcels to go around the postbox, and it would be fun to pipe or paint the names of the party guests on the individual envelopes.

Ingredients

quantity for 23cm (9inch) square madeira cake (p.12)
175g (6oz) buttercream (p.15)
45ml (3tbsp) raspberry jam
900g (2lb) fondant icing (p.13)
apricot glaze (p.15)
225g (8oz) royal icing (p.13)
food colourings: red, black, green
icing sugar or cornflour for dusting

Materials and decoration

23cm (9inch) square cake drum
cocktail stick
length of purple ribbon

Equipment

two 850g (1lb14oz) empty food cans, both ends removed
non-stick paper
baking tray
paint brush
piping bag with fine writing (No.1) nozzle
palette knife

Note: *Allow an extra day or overnight preparation time for icing to set.*

Method

1 Line both the empty food cans with greased non-stick paper. Divide the cake mixture between the cans and place on a greased baking tray. Bake for about 1 hour 20 minutes in a 170°C (325°F/Gas Mark 3) oven, before turning out and cooling on a wire rack.

2 Trim the top of one of the cakes so that it is flat. Cut each cake into three equal portions horizontally, and sandwich them together again with the buttercream and jam. You should then have one cylindrical cake, six pieces high.

3 Measure the height of the cake and its circumference, and cut out a piece of non-stick paper to a rectangle of these dimensions. Wrap this piece of paper around the cake to check it covers it accurately.

4 Colour three-quarters of the fondant (about 675g/1½lb) with red food colouring. (Keep the rest tightly wrapped to prevent drying out.) Take two-thirds of the red fondant – about 450g (1lb) – and roll it out thinly on a surface dusted with icing sugar or cornflour to the size of the paper rectangle. Trim it to fit exactly and brush with apricot glaze. Carefully wrap the fondant around the cake, rolling it on with the paper to help you. Press the fondant into shape.

5 Carefully lift the cake into a vertical position and secure flat side down on the cake drum with royal icing.

6 Take about half the remaining red fondant (100g/4oz) and roll it to a very thick strip, about 1cm (½inch) deep and wide. Trim the edges so they are straight and even, and cut the strip so that it measures the circumference of the cake. Fix around the postbox to form a 'collar', and score lightly with the back of a knife.

7 Smooth and fill any cracks or pits on top of the cake with spare pieces of fondant to give a smooth, rounded surface. Roll out the remaining red fondant to a circle a little larger than the cake and use to cover the top of the postbox, overlapping the fondant 'collar' slightly all the way round. Score the bottom edge lightly with the back of a knife.

8 Keep back some of the remaining white fondant (about 75g/3oz) and colour the rest with black food colouring. Roll the black fondant out on a surface dusted with cornflour or icing sugar to a strip about 5cm (2inches) wide and as long as the circumference of the cake. It should be about 5mm (¼inch) thick. Trim the strip so that it is even, and wrap around the base of the postbox, using a dampened paint brush and smoothing over the join.

9 Using red fondant trimmings, shape a long-wedged piece for the little hood over the postbox opening. Position on with a little water.

10 Roll out the remaining white fondant and cut out a little rectangle for the collection-time sign. Secure on to the front of the postbox. Cut out envelope shapes and an oval for the top sign, and leave to dry on non-stick paper for about 24 hours.

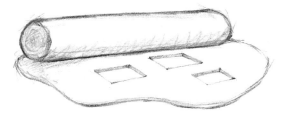

11 The next day, colour a little royal icing black and place in a piping bag with a fine writing nozzle. Pipe names and/or addresses on the envelopes, and times of collection on the timetable notice. Pipe the words TO THE POST OFFICE on the oval sign, with an arrow.

12 Secure the oval plaque on top of the postbox using a little black fondant as a holder. Prop up with a cocktail stick from behind if necessary. Lay the envelopes around the base of the postbox.

13 Colour the remaining royal icing green (keeping a little back for the flowers if liked) and cover the drum around the postbox, peaking with a palette knife for a grass effect. If liked, white and yellow daisies can be piped on to the grass. Finally, wrap the ribbon around the edge of the cake drum, securing with glue or royal icing.

Jolly Clown

C olourful and cheery, this sitting-up clown should appeal to younger children especially. The plump body of the clown is made from partly-filled pudding basins to give the shallow domes required. To add birthday candles, make little holes all around the edge of the cake drum.

Ingredients

quantity for 20cm (8inch) round chocolate-flavoured quick sponge cake (p.8)
15ml (1tbsp) lemon jelly marmalade
900g (2lb) fondant icing (p.13)
2 brown Smarties
food colourings: yellow, brown, green, red, blue
icing sugar or cornflour for dusting
Materials and decoration
20cm (8inch) square cake drum
length of yellow ribbon
Equipment
1.1ltr (2pint) ovenproof pudding basin
two 450ml (¾pint) ovenproof pudding basins
non-stick paper
paint brush

Method

1 Grease and line the base of the large 1.1ltr (2pint) basin and the two small 450ml (¾pint) basins with greased non-stick paper. Half fill the small basins with cake mixture and fill the large basin with the remainder. Bake at 170°C (325°F/Gas Mark 3), allowing 40 minutes for the cakes baked in the small basins and 55 minutes for the cake baked in the large basin. Turn out on to a wire rack and leave to cool completely.

2 Melt the lemon jelly marmalade with 15ml (1tbsp) water in a saucepan. Cut a little off the wide base of the large cake so that it will sit firmly as the domed body of the clown. Cut the risen surfaces off the small cakes and sandwich these together with the marmalade to form the head. Brush the entire surfaces of all the cakes with the remaining marmalade.

3 Colour a small piece of fondant icing, about 100g (4oz) with yellow food colouring. Dampen the cake drum with water. Roll out half the yellow fondant as thinly as possible to a 20cm (8inch) square on a surface dusted with icing sugar or cornflour. Transfer to the drum to cover, and trim the edges. Reserve the trimmings, tightly wrapped.

4 Take three small pieces of fondant, each weighing about 100g (4oz). Colour one piece brown, one green and leave the remainder white. Divide the remaining icing in half, and colour one piece red and one blue. (Keep unused icing tightly wrapped.)

5 Roll out three-quarters of the red icing – about 175g (6oz) – to an area that will cover half the large cake. Trim one edge neatly with a knife so that it is straight – the straight edge should be about 30cm (12inches) long. Cover half the large cake so that the cut edge runs over the centre of the 'body'. Roll out the same amount of blue fondant to a similarly sized area and use to cover the remaining half of the body in the same way. Place on the cake drum.

6 Roll out three-quarters of the white icing to a 20cm (8inch) circle and use to cover the clown's head, tucking the ends under. Secure the head to the body with a dampened brush.

7 Shape the remaining white icing into hands and feet. Secure the feet with a dampened brush to the front of the cake. Roll out more red icing to a semi-circle, about 7.5cm (3inches) along the straight side. Lightly brush the surface with water. Lay a 'hand' on one side of the semi-circle, and bring the semi-circle over the hand to form a sleeve. Keeping one end of the sleeve open, secure it to the blue side of the body. Cover the other arm in blue icing in the same way, and attach to the red side of the body.

8 To make hair, roll the piece of brown icing to a number of long thin sausages and cut each into 2.5cm (1inch) lengths. Dampen the hair area of head with a little water and secure the strips in place.

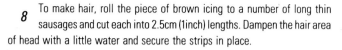

9 Next, shape the green icing (keeping a little back for the buttons) into a cone, and position on the head for the hat. Cut out small rounds of green icing for buttons and secure on the front of the body.

10 Roll out a circle of red icing and slice into eight 5mm (¼inch) strips. Secure as stripes on the appropriate sleeves (red on blue, and vice versa). Roll out the remaining yellow icing into two curved strips, about 2.5×12.5cm (1×5inches), trim the edges and secure around the neck for a collar.

11 Position a small blob of red icing on the face for a nose, and cut out and press on a smily mouth. Position two ovals of blue icing for eyes and press a Smartie into each. Use the remaining icing to complete the facial features and to add pockets and a bow tie. Finally, wrap the ribbon round the edge of the board, securing it at the back with a blob of icing.

Fairground Carousel

Although there isn't much sponge cake in this recipe, it is quite complicated to make and requires a little patience and careful measuring. To make it easier, you could buy little marzipan animals instead of moulding them yourself – however, if you do make your own, it might be fun to make them in the shape of the children's pets and pipe their names on to them.

Ingredients

18cm (7inch) deep round Victoria sponge cake (p.9)

apricot glaze (p.15)

450g (1lb) marzipan (p.14)

900g (2lb) fondant icing (p.13)

225g (8oz) royal icing (p.13)

12 striped candy canes

6 marzipan animals (home-made or bought)

225g (8oz) sweets (optional)

food colourings: red, blue, gold

icing sugar or cornflour for dusting

Materials and decoration

two 25cm (10inch) hexagonal cake drums

aluminium foil

coloured paper

length of blue ribbon

7 cocktail sticks

Equipment

non-stick paper

piping bag with small star (No.27) nozzle

paint brush

Note: Allow an extra day or overnight preparation time for icing to set.

Method

1 Brush the cake with apricot glaze. Roll out the marzipan on a surface dusted with icing sugar or cornflour to a large circle (about 25cm/10inches). Cover the top and sides of the cake with the marzipan, press on and trim away excess around the base.

2 Divide the fondant in two and colour one half red and one blue. Keep the blue fondant tightly wrapped to prevent drying out and roll out half the red fondant (about 225g/8oz) to a long strip as wide as the height of the cake and as long as its circumference. Wrap the strip around the sides of the cake, trimming away excess and smoothing over the join.

3 Roll out the remaining red fondant to a 14.2×29cm (5⁶⁄₁₀×11²⁄₅inch) rect-angle. Cut this into three triangles (see illustration) and leave on non-stick paper to dry overnight.

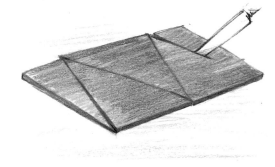

4 Meanwhile, roll out half the blue fondant (about 225g/8oz) into a rect-angle of the same size and cut out three identical triangles. Leave to dry.

5 Roll out the remaining blue fondant to a large circle about 27.5cm (11inches) and use to cover one cake drum, securing with a little royal icing. Place the red cake centrally on top of the blue base, securing with a little icing or water.

6 Using scissors, cut out six 'mirrors' from foil and attach them evenly around the sides of the cake using dabs of royal icing. Place a little icing in a piping bag with a star nozzle and pipe a decorative border around each foil mirror. Leave to dry overnight.

7 The next day, make six holes at equal intervals around the top edge of the blue cake drum to accommodate the candy canes. With a sharp instrument, make six corresponding holes in the bottom of the second cake drum (the 'roof'). Place six of the canes in the base holes and fit the roof on top so that it sits on top of the cake.

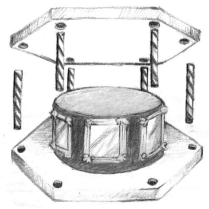

8 Using a brush, paint the piped borders around the mirrors with gold colouring. Insert a candy cane into the centre of each marzipan animal and place each one on the blue base in front of a mirror, securing the canes to the roof with a little royal icing or fondant. If you like, you could pipe children's names on to each animal too.

9 Roll out a small ball of fondant or marzipan trimmings and place it centrally on top of the roof drum to act as a support for the triangles. Then, using royal icing as cement, carefully lay the coloured triangles, red and blue alternately, beside each other to form a pointed roof. If liked, fill the cavity with little sweets before placing on the final triangle. Place a little royal icing in a piping bag with a star nozzle and pipe along the joins of the triangles to secure them. Allow to dry for a few hours before painting with gold food colouring.

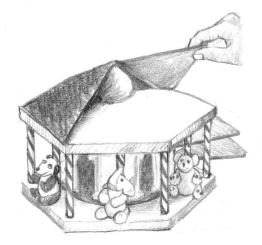

10 Cut out a long strip of coloured paper and cut a scalloped edge along one side. Sticking on with a little royal icing or glue, wrap the strip carefully around the edge of the roof, scalloped edge upwards. Secure the blue ribbon around the base of the carousel.

11 Make six little flags and one larger one out of cocktail sticks and triangles of coloured paper. Attach six around the roof at equal intervals and place the seventh in the centre at the top. The carousel could, if desired, be placed on an inexpensive cake turntable to achieve a lovely 'spinning' effect.

Pop-up Birthday Card

*D*on't be put off by the delicate appearance of this cake, but do allow plenty of time for the separate pieces of icing to harden well before assembling them all together. Any combination of colours can be used to suit your own taste, but avoid too many or the general appearance may become confused and be less attractive.

Ingredients

15cm (6inch) square rich fruit cake (p.11)

1.5kg (3lb) fondant icing (p.13)

apricot glaze (p.15)

225g (8oz) royal icing (p.13)

food colourings; green, pink, violet

icing sugar or cornflour for dusting

Materials and decoration

20cm (8inch) square cake drum

shiny paper or piece of cloth

sticky tape

length of pink ribbon

candles

Equipment

non-stick paper

firm white card (A3 size)

aluminium foil

lightweight saw or sturdy knife

paint brush

piping bag with medium writing (No.2) nozzle and small star (No.27) nozzle

Note: *Allow at least 3 days extra preparation time for icing to set.*

Method

1 Trace the templates (see overleaf) on to non-stick paper, then re-trace the outlines only on to pieces of firm card so that you have a paper and card template of each shape. Cut out templates.

2 Roll out half the fondant icing on a surface dusted with icing sugar or cornflour to 5mm (¼inch) thickness. Gently rest the card templates over the icing and cut around. Transfer the icing cut-outs to a sheet of foil or non-stick paper, and rest the 'birthday cake' cut-out on a piece of foil wrapped around a cake tin, so that it sets into a curved shape. Leave to dry out for at least 48 hours.

3 Cut the cake drum in half diagonally using a lightweight saw or sturdy knife. Place one half on top of the other to form one large triangle, and stick together with sticky tape. Cover the entire drum with paper or cloth, and wrap the ribbon around the drum, securing with glue or royal icing.

4 Cut the rich fruit cake in half diagonally and place one half on top of the other to form a triangle, sandwiching on with a little apricot glaze. Brush the remaining glaze over the rest of the cake and place on the cake drum.

5 Colour the remaining fondant with green food colouring and roll out to a triangle, about 32.5cm (13inches) on the long side and 25cm (10inches) on the short. Use to cover the triangular cake, smoothing the icing around the sides with your hands (first dusted with icing sugar or cornflour). Trim off excess icing around the base.

6 Trace the dotted lines on the paper templates on to the hardened icing cut-outs. (Do this by pencilling over the side of the paper, turning it over on to the icing and then pressing gently over the lines again.) Using a fine paint brush, decorate the cut-outs in appropriate colours, pink and violet perhaps. If liked, add a written message under (or instead of) the HAPPY BIRTHDAY. Leave to dry out for several hours.

7 Carefully peel the backing foil or paper off the icing cut-outs. Place a little royal icing in a piping bag fitted with a medium writing (No.2) nozzle. Pipe a line of icing along the lower and centre edges of the 'card' (left) and 'card' (right). Secure them to the top of the cake in an open card position, holding the card in place until it feels sufficiently stable.

8 Pipe royal icing along the short sides of the 'birthday cake' cut-out. Gently attach to the card, resting the base on a matchbox to raise the cake slightly off the green fondant. Pipe more icing around the edges of the 'balloons' cut-out and secure with a blob of royal icing to the card behind the birthday cake. Place a jar underneath to hold it up until it dries. Pipe more icing along the bases of the 'parcels' and 'party hats' cut-outs, and attach to the green icing in front of the 'birthday cake'. Leave to set for 24 hours.

9 Using the medium writing nozzle, make loops of icing joining the base of each balloon to the card. Make more loops around the birthday cake and the base of the cake. Pipe bows on to the parcels and decorate the party hats. Place the remaining royal icing in the piping bag and fit with a small star nozzle. Pipe rosettes around the top of the birthday cake, and gently press the appropriate number of candles into the rosettes.

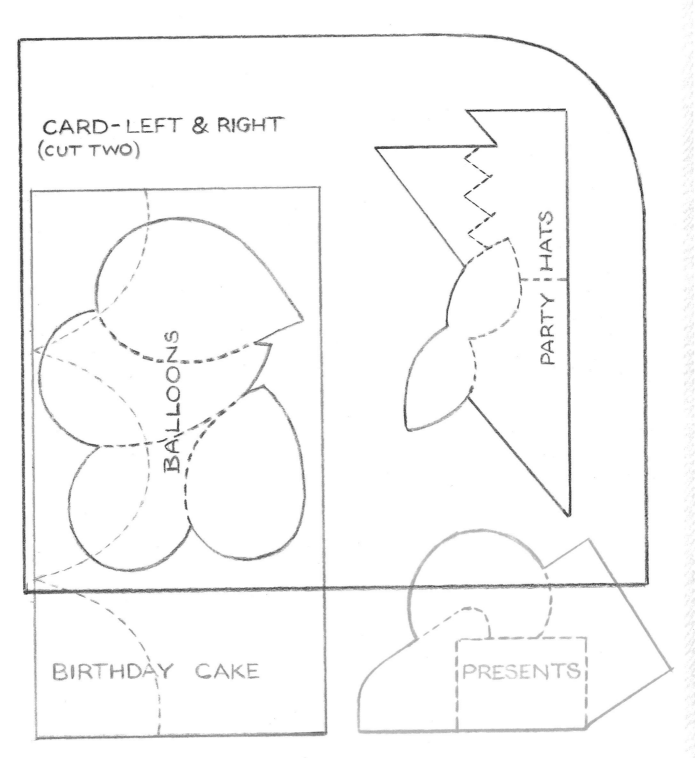

CARD-LEFT & RIGHT
(CUT TWO)

BALLOONS

PARTY HATS

BIRTHDAY CAKE

PRESENTS

Octopus in Top Hat

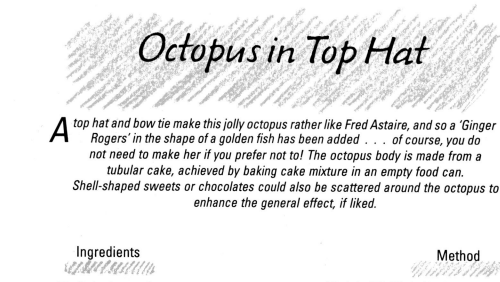

A top hat and bow tie make this jolly octopus rather like Fred Astaire, and so a 'Ginger Rogers' in the shape of a golden fish has been added . . . of course, you do not need to make her if you prefer not to! The octopus body is made from a tubular cake, achieved by baking cake mixture in an empty food can. Shell-shaped sweets or chocolates could also be scattered around the octopus to enhance the general effect, if liked.

Ingredients

75g (3oz) soft margarine
75g (3oz) caster sugar
2 eggs (size 3)
100g (4oz) self-raising flour
1.25ml (¼tsp) baking powder
2.5ml (½tsp) ground mixed spice
75g (3oz) mixed dried fruit
15ml (1tbsp) milk
900g (2lb) fondant icing (p.13)
apricot glaze (p.15)
100g (4oz) desiccated coconut
food colourings: blue, black, orange, yellow, red, green, silver (optional)
icing sugar or cornflour for dusting

Materials and decoration

candles
25cm (10inch) round gold cake drum
length of blue ribbon (optional)

Equipment

800g (1lb12oz) empty food can, both ends removed
baking tray
non-stick paper
paint brush

Method

1. Wash the 800g (1lb12oz) food can thoroughly. Stand the can on a baking tray and line its base and sides with greased non-stick paper.

2. Place the margarine, sugar, egg, flour, baking powder and spice in a bowl. Beat well until smooth. Beat in the mixed dried fruit and milk and turn into the prepared can. Bake at 180°C (350°F/Gas Mark 4) for about 45 minutes or until a skewer inserted in the centre comes out clean. Leave in the tin for 10 minutes then turn out and transfer to a wire rack to cool completely.

3. Using a sharp knife, cut a 'waist' into the cake about a third of the way up. If the top of the cake is fairly flat, trim the edges with a knife to round the top of the head.

Note: *Allow at least 3 extra days preparation time for icing to set.*

4 Reserve (tightly wrapped) a smallish ball of white fondant and colour the remainder blue. Divide in two and store half (tightly wrapped) to cover the body later. Cut the other half into eight equal pieces for the tentacles. To shape a tentacle, roll one piece on a surface dusted with icing sugar or cornflour to a thick sausage about 15cm (6inches) long, tapering to a point at one end. Bend into a curve and transfer to non-stick paper. Wrap a candle in the end of each tentacle, leaving one for the cane, if preferred. Make the other tentacles in the same way, varying the direction of the curve so that when assembled the tentacles branch out at different angles. (Leave some tentacles without candles if less are required.) Leave to dry for 48 hours or more.

5 Brush the cake with apricot glaze and place the cake on the cake drum. Roll out all the remaining blue fondant to a 25cm (10inch) circle and use to cover the cake, easing to fit and smoothing the icing around the sides of the cake with hands dusted with icing sugar or cornflour. Trim off excess icing around the base.

6 While the icing is still soft dampen the ends of the tentacles and press them, one at a time, around the base of the cake. Cover the joins with thin ribbons of blue fondant if necessary. Leave to harden for 24 hours, supporting them with small items such as matchboxes if necessary.

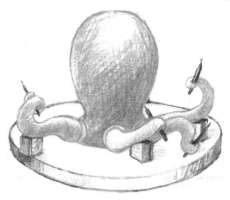

7 At the same time, mould a black top hat, bow tie and cane, and an orange fish if liked from some of the reserved fondant. Leave to dry on non-stick paper.

8 Use the remaining white icing to shape the eyes and mouth, and position on the octopus' face. (If liked, mould eyes and a bow for the little fish as well, and press on.)

9 When dry, and using a fine paint brush, paint the eyes and mouth yellow and red. Paint on other facial features and the suckers on the tentacles with black colouring. You could also paint the tip of the cane silver, if liked. Finally, colour the desiccated coconut blue or green and scatter over the cake drum.

10 If liked, wrap the ribbon around the edge of the drum and secure with glue or royal icing.

Speed Cruiser

*his bright and colourful boat is rather larger than most speed boats, but feeds
more children that way! The windscreen in front of the 'cabin' looks just like
glass, but is in fact edible and made out of melted glacier mint – a clever and
original idea you could adapt for other cakes, for example for windows.*

Ingredients

24×30cm (9½×12inch) rectangular madeira cake (p.12)

175g (6oz) buttercream (p.15)

900g (2lb) fondant icing (p.13)

675g (1½lb) royal icing (p.13)

1–2 glacier mints

food colourings: blue, red, pink, black, silver, brown, green

icing sugar or cornflour for dusting

Materials and decoration

38cm (15inch) square cake drum

1 straw

10 cocktail sticks, shaped variety if preferred

length of blue ribbon

Equipment

non-stick paper

paint brush

piping bag with fine writing (No.1) nozzle

baking tray

palette knife

Note: *Allow an extra day or overnight preparation time for icing to set.*

Method

1   Slice the cake lengthwise into two halves to give two long, thin cakes.
Trim the top of one cake flat and place the other cake on top of it. Holding firm with one hand, cut and shape the cake as illustrated. Carve both from the top in a boat shape, and from the side to give the round hull.

2   Cut out a small square from the top of the boat, near the squared end. It should be about 5cm (2inches) square and 2.5cm (1inch) deep.

3   Sandwich the different parts of the boat together with buttercream and then spread the remaining buttercream over the entire cake.

4   Take about three-quarters of the fondant (about 675g/1½lb) and roll out to a large area. Cover the boat with the fondant, pressing around the corners and smoothing on. Trim away the icing from the carved hole and excess from around the base. Transfer the boat to the cake drum and secure on with a little royal icing.

5 Colour a tiny piece of fondant blue and mould it into a 5cm (2inch) rounded bench to fit into the back of the cabin area. Press into the hole in the boat. Colour some fondant red, about 50g (2oz), and roll out. Cut out long thin strips for trimming around the top edge of the boat and fix on with a dampened paint brush. Cut out a thicker decorative strip for the deck (perhaps with a forked end) and press into place. At the same time, mould two balls of red fondant for the buoys and leave to dry on non-stick paper. Cut out numerals of red (a set for each side of the boat) and also leave to dry.

6 Cut out two tiny rectangular panels for the plates on each side of the boat and press on, securing with a little water or royal icing.

7 Reserving about a third for the piping work later, place the royal icing in a piping bag with a fine writing nozzle. Pipe outlines of sixteen lifebelts on to non-stick paper – inner and outer circles, with a hole about 2.5cm (1inch) in diameter. Then, pipe or spoon inside the outlines so that icing floods into a tyre shape. Leave to dry overnight until hard. At the same time, pipe an anchor on to non-stick paper and leave to dry.

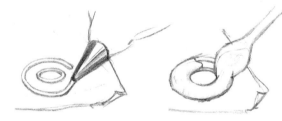

8 Take a piece of non-stick paper and mark on with a pencil an outline for a 5cm (2inch) long and 2cm (¾inch) deep rectangle, for the windscreen. Place the glacier mint(s) within the windscreen area and then carefully place the paper with the mint on to a baking tray. Bake in a preheated 180°C (350°F/ Gas Mark 4) oven until melted, about 5 minutes. Be careful not to let it bubble. Take out the paper and leave to cool slightly, shaping frequently with a palette knife to retain the windscreen shape. When the windscreen is cool but still flexible, wrap it (still on its paper) around a large glass jar so that it cools completely into a gentle curved shape. Once cooled, peel off the paper carefully and fix the 'glass' windscreen on to the boat, securing on with royal icing.

9 Colour pieces of the remaining fondant icing (and using any trimmings) to make the sailor – fleshy pink, blue and a little white. Mould his head and upper torso, and leave to dry overnight on non-stick paper. (Alternatively, you could mould the figure from white fondant and paint in appropriate colours using a paint brush and food colouring once dry.) Paint on facial features and, when dry, place inside the passenger area. Add a black steering wheel.

10 Make flags for the buoys and boat by cutting out triangles of paper, one large and two small. For the large flag, paint a straw with silver food colouring and when dry, glue on to the large paper triangle. For the smaller flags, glue on to halved cocktail sticks and stick into the red balls of fondant. Place the buoys on the cake drum around the boat and stick the large flag on to the back of the boat with a little royal icing.

11 When dry, unpeel the lifebelt shapes gently and stick two together, back to back, to form eight rounded lifebelts. Allow to dry a little. Paint the anchor with silver food colouring and place on the deck. Secure the red numbers on to the side panels with royal icing, and then fix the lifebelts on to the boat in the same way, three on each side and two on the deck.

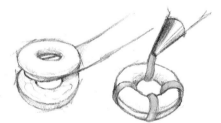

12 To make the railings, press halved cocktail sticks point down into the icing at 2cm (¾inch) intervals all the way round the front edge of the deck – about eighteen in all. Colour a little royal icing brown and place in a piping bag with a writing nozzle. Pipe loops carefully along the railings all the way round, and allow to dry. At the same time pipe ropes on to the lifebelts and for the anchor.

13 Keeping a little white icing back for the wave crests, tint the remaining royal icing shades of different blues and greens for the sea. Spread it over the cake drum around the boat and buoys with a palette knife, blending the different tones together and making sure that the fondant under the boat is covered.

14 Pipe the remaining white icing over the sea to make little crests on the waves. Finally, wrap the ribbon around the edge of the cake drum, securing on with a little spare royal icing.

Sunbathing Teddy Bear

*A*ny number of appropriate accessories can be moulded from fondant icing for this
cool character – perhaps some fizzy pop in a can could be added,
or a magazine. When piling the buttercream on to the teddy's body,
try to mound it up quite high to give him a tubby appearance.
Because the cake is covered in buttercream it will not keep so long as
cakes made with fondant, so eat it fairly soon after it is made.

Ingredients

*20cm (8inch) square sandwich chocolate-flavoured Victoria sponge
cake (p.9)*

900g (2lb) fondant icing (p.13)

225g (8oz) chocolate buttercream (p.15)

225g (8oz) royal icing (p.13)

food colourings: yellow, blue, green, red, silver

icing sugar or cornflour for dusting

Materials and decoration

25cm (10inch) square cake drum

Equipment

paint brush

palette knife

2 cocktail sticks

piping bag with fine writing (No.1) nozzle

Method

1 Cut a 6.5cm (2½inch) wide strip off one side of the cake. From this strip slice off a 6.5cm (2½inch) length for the teddy's body and a 4cm (1½inch) length for the head. (The remaining part of the 'strip' is not used.) Round off the edges of the body and head.

2 Place the large piece of cake on the cake drum. Colour half the fondant icing (about 450g/1lb) with yellow food colouring. Roll this out on a surface dusted with icing sugar or cornflour to a large rectangle and use to cover the large cake. Trim off icing around the base, but let it still cover the drum slightly.

3 Thinly roll a rectangle of white fondant for the towel (10×16.5cm/4×6½inches), trim and position on top of the cake. Brightly paint the towel using blue and green food colourings and a fine paint brush. Leave the fondant to dry slightly.

Snakes & Ladders

*T*his cake is very effective and yet is simple to make as it is based on a straight-forward square cake. Follow the photograph or your own set of Snakes & Ladders for the exact layout of the different coloured squares. The snakes are made from rolled-up pieces of multi-coloured fondant, but you could use bought jelly snakes instead to save time if preferred.

Ingredients

25cm (10inch) square madeira cake (p.12)

175g (6oz) chocolate buttercream (p.15)

225g (8oz) royal icing (p.13)

apricot glaze (p.15)

900g (2lb) fondant icing (p.13)

food colourings: yellow, red, blue, green, black, brown

icing sugar or cornflour for dusting

Materials and decoration

30cm (12inch) square cake drum

Equipment

non-stick paper

piping bag with medium writing (No.2) nozzle and fine writing (No.1) nozzle

Note: *Allow an extra day or overnight preparation time for icing to set.*

Method

1 Cut the cake in half horizontally and sandwich together again with the chocolate buttercream. Secure the cake to the cake drum (with a little royal icing) and brush all over with apricot glaze.

2 Colour three-quarters of the fondant (about 675g/1½lb) with yellow food colouring. (Keep the rest tightly wrapped to prevent drying out.) Roll out half the yellow fondant on a surface dusted with icing sugar or corn-flour to a large square about 35cm (14inches) across. Carefully transfer the fon-dant to the cake (using your arms and hands dusted with icing sugar to support it) and cover, smoothing over. Square off the corners and edges neatly.

3 Roll out the other half of yellow fondant on non-stick paper to a 25cm (10inch) square and trim the edges evenly. Divide the square into 49 little squares with a knife by marking six evenly-spaced lines vertically and six horizontally. Separate slightly and leave to dry, about 24 hours. Roll out the trimmings to four long strips and cover the cake drum around the cake.

4 At the same time, and keeping a tiny amount of white fondant in reserve for the dice, divide the remaining fondant into four even portions (about 50g/2oz each). Colour one piece red, one blue, one green and one black. Keep the black fondant back, tightly wrapped, until later. Roll out the red, blue and green fondant separately on non-stick paper, each to an area the same thickness as the little yellow squares. Cut out two blue squares, eight red squares and eight green squares – all the same size as the yellow squares. Leave them all to dry for 24 hours. (Reserve all the fondant trimmings, tightly wrapped, for later use.)

5 Colour a little royal icing brown and place in a piping bag with a medium writing nozzle. Pipe ladders on to non-stick paper, and leave them to harden.

6 The next day, brush the top of the cake slightly with a little water. Replacing eighteen of the yellow squares with the other coloured squares, arrange them neatly on the cake to form the game board. (Follow the photograph for the exact layout of different colours.)

7 Take the reserved black fondant. Roll out and cut out four strips about 25cm (10inches) long and 2.5cm (1inch) wide, and secure around the edge of the cake to form a rim.

8 Gather up the red, blue, green and yellow fondant trimmings, keep a little piece of each aside for the counters, and then press together. Taking one multi-coloured piece at a time, roll out long tubes with your fingers for snakes. Trim and shape the heads and tails, and bend the snakes appro-

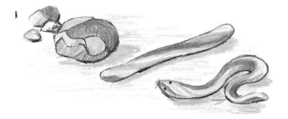

priately. Place the snakes on the game board, making sure that the head and tail of each snake are on squares of the same colour. Round counters can then be formed from different colours, and two cubes for the dice made from the reserved piece of white fondant.

9 Place some royal icing in a piping bag with a medium writing nozzle and pipe thin white lines between each square on the game board. Colour the remaining royal icing black, and place in a bag with a fine writing nozzle. Pipe the words START and FINISH on to the top left and bottom right squares, and then pipe numbers on to the squares in consecutive order. Pipe black dots on to the dice.

10 Finally, place the ladders on the board carefully, making sure that they start and end on squares of the same colour. Place the dice and counters around the board.

Mummy in Sarcophagus

This cake is for those with a sense of the macabre, or a love for the old Hammer Horror films. The sarcophagus can be decorated in as much detail as you like, and could be painted quite elaborately. Jelly snakes have been added for a 'desert' feel, or perhaps you could add a toy rubber tarantula or scorpion.

Ingredients

20×25×7.5cm (8×10×3inch) deep rectangular Victoria sponge cake (p.9)

apricot glaze (p.15)

450g (1lb) marzipan (p.14)

675g (1½lb) fondant icing (p.13)

food colourings: yellow, black, and other bright colours of choice

icing sugar or cornflour for dusting

Materials and decoration

32.5cm (13inch) round cake drum

2 sheets of medium sandpaper

glue

length of yellow ribbon

jelly snakes (optional)

Equipment

modelling tools or printing sticks

cocktail stick

paint brush

Note: *Allow an extra day or overnight preparation time for icing to set.*

Method

1 Slice the cake in half lengthways to form two long thin cakes. Carve each half into a curved 'sarcophagus' shape as shown in the illustration below.

2 Carve one half so that it is mounded at one end and tapering at the other, to form the lid (see illustration). Cut a small wedge from cake trimmings and attach to the bottom end of the lid half.

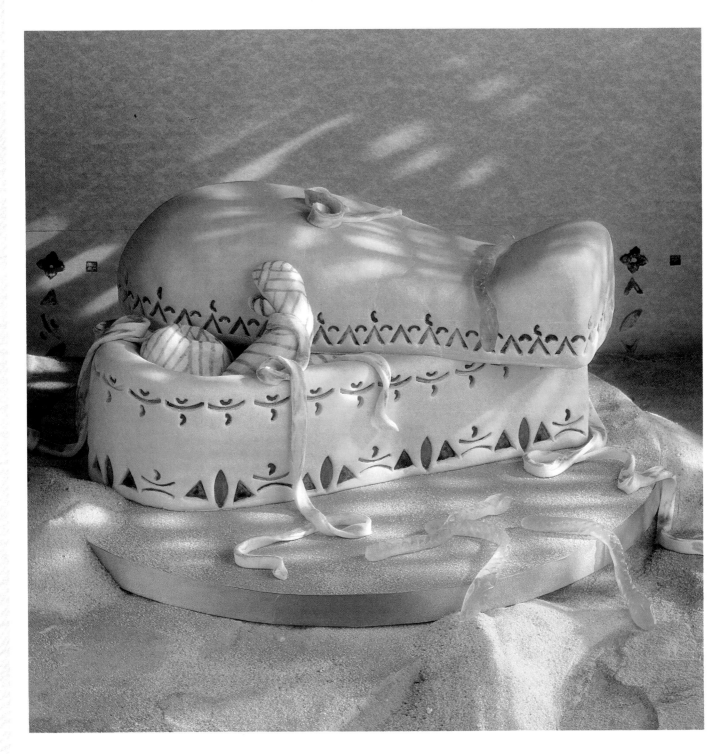

3 Hollow out the other half of cake to form the sarcophagus base, leaving a rim of at least 1cm (½inch) all the way around, and carving out to about half the depth. Brush all over the outside and inside with apricot glaze. Roll out the marzipan on a surface dusted with icing sugar or cornflour into a large rectangle and use to cover the base, smoothing into the hollow and over the corners, and trimming away excess from around the bottom.

4 Cover the top of the cake drum with the sandpaper, securing it with glue and trimming to fit. (You will have to cut and join the paper.)

5 Colour two-thirds of the fondant icing (about 450g/1lb) yellowy-cream and roll out to two large rectangles of the same dimensions as the marzipan. Use to cover the base and the lid of the sarcophagus, easing into the corners and hollow. Trim away excess and place the base on to the cake drum.

6 Using modelling tools, print sticks or the ends of pens, press decorative borders into the fondant around and all over the cake base and lid.

7 Colour the remaining fondant with tiny amount of black food colouring to give a dirty grey shade. Use this to model an Egyptian mummy's head and shoulders, and an arm with a hand. Mark lines of bandages on to the mummy's limbs and head with a pointed cocktail stick. Cut thin strips of greyish fondant for bandages, and keep wrapped in cling film to prevent drying out.

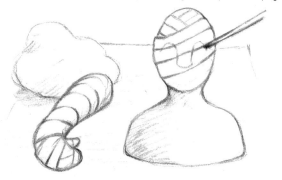

8 Place the mummy's head in the sarcophagus at the appropriate end. Position the sarcophagus lid on to the base, so that it is open at an angle – use a cocktail stick inserted into the corner to help secure the lid if necessary. Attach the arm inside the sarcophagus so that it looks as if it is coming out of the base, and bend it up slightly so that it looks as if it is pushing up the lid. Attach a 'bandage' to the arm and drape over the sarcophagus to look as if it is unravelling. Trail more bandages over the sarcophagus to enhance the effect. Leave to dry for a few hours or overnight.

9 When the sarcophagus is dry, paint the decoration and indentations in bright colours, and add little touches of black outline to define the mummy's bandages. Wrap the ribbon around the edge of the cake drum, securing with glue. Finally, drape jelly snakes over and around the sarcophagus if liked for extra effect.

Green Dragon

There's nothing very scary about this sleepy green dragon – although you could scatter gold chocolate coins around for him to 'guard' if you like. The basic shape is very easy to make, but if you do have a little time you might want to give the dragon more elaborate scales. Pipe decorative scales over him in different colours, or paint their edges with gold and silver food colouring.

Ingredients

25cm (10inch) deep round Victoria sponge cake (p.9)

450g (1lb) fondant icing (p.13)

apricot glaze (p.15)

675g (1½lb) marzipan (p.14)

100g (4oz) royal icing (p.13)

green and yellow lustre powder (optional)

food colourings: yellow, orange, green, red, black

icing sugar or cornflour for dusting

Materials and decoration

30cm (12inch) round cake drum

length of brown or red ribbon

Equipment

non-stick paper

piping bag with tiny writing (No.0.5) nozzle

paint brush

Note: *Allow an extra day or overnight preparation time for icing to set.*

Method

1 Colour half the fondant with yellow and a little orange food colouring to create a slightly marbled effect and roll out on a surface dusted with icing sugar or cornflour to a large circle. Use to cover the cake drum, smoothing over and trimming away excess around the base.

2 Level the top of the cake and cut in half vertically to form two semi-circles. Brush the top of one semi-circle with apricot glaze and place the other on top to form a half-moon sandwich. Turn over carefully and place, cut side down, on the cake drum. This will form the dragon's body.

3 Using a sharp knife, shave a little off the sides of the body to round off the edges slightly. Brush all over with apricot glaze.

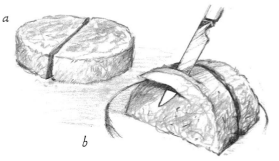

a

b

4 Colour the marzipan a bright green and roll out a third (about 225g/8oz) on a surface dusted with icing sugar or cornflour to a large circle. (Keep the unused marzipan tightly wrapped until needed.) Use the circle to cover the dragon's body, smoothing it over the curves and trimming away excess around the base.

5 Using half the remaining marzipan (225g/8oz), model a long tail and attach it to the back of the body, smoothing over the join with your fingers. Use the remaining marzipan to model a head with a long neck. Press it into the side opposite the tail and bend both around to meet each other.

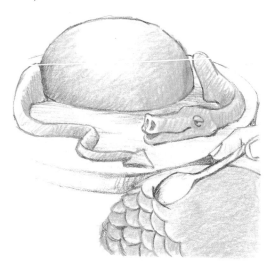

6 Using the edge of a teaspoon, mark scales all over the body of the dragon, including the neck, head and tail.

7 Take a tiny piece of fondant, colour it red and cut out a forked tongue. Leave to dry on non-stick paper. Colour the remaining fondant icing three different shades of green. Roll out each portion and cut out various sizes of triangle from each, enough to form 'fins' to go along the dragon's back and tail. Place them, spaced well apart, on non-stick paper and leave to dry overnight.

8 The next day, push the fins into the marzipan, starting at the head with the smaller triangles, getting larger over the back of the body, and then smaller towards the tip of the tail.

9 Place royal icing in a piping bag with a tiny nozzle and pipe eyes and fangs on to the head. Attach the tongue in the mouth using a little royal icing to secure. Paint an eyeball and the line of the dragon's smile with black food colouring.

10 Finally, glue a ribbon around the edge of the drum and brush the dragon with a little lustre powder if desired to give the scales a shiny effect.

Paintbox & Brushes

This is a colourful cake that is relatively simple to make as it is based on a flat rectangular sponge cake. Don't worry if you find that the fondant does not line the holes for the paint blocks neatly – the blocks could always be made with piped squares of coloured royal icing. A good cake for a child with artistic ambitions . . .

Ingredients

24×30cm (9½×12inch) rectangular madeira cake (p.12)

apricot glaze (p.15)

900g (2lb) fondant icing (p.13)

225g (8oz) royal icing (p.13)

food colourings: blue, brown, black, silver, and other colours of choice

icing sugar or cornflour for dusting

Materials and decoration

38cm (15inch) square cake drum

length of pale ribbon

Equipment

non-stick paper

piping bag with medium writing (No.2) nozzle

waxed paper

paint brush

Note: *Allow at least 1 day extra preparation time for icing to set.*

Method

1 Cut a thin v-shaped wedge along the centre of the cake widthways, about halfway down into the sponge. This is to separate the paintbox base from its lid.

2 Carve two rows of four small rectangular holes on one half of the cake (the paintbox base), evenly spaced apart. Hollow out the other side of the cake (the lid) so that there is an even 2cm (¾inch) border all around. The hollow should be about halfway down into the sponge. Place the paintbox on the cake drum, and brush all over with apricot glaze.

3 Roll out two-thirds of the fondant (about 575g/1¼lb) on a surface dusted with icing sugar or cornflour. Roll it to a rectangle a little larger than the entire cake, about 32.5×38cm (13×15inches). Using your hands and arms dusted with icing sugar to support the fondant, carefully drape it over the cake. Keeping one hand under the fondant for support, smooth it over the top of the cake with your other hand, easing the icing into all the hollows and indentations. Smooth and fit the icing around the corners before smoothing down the sides. Trim off the excess with a knife.

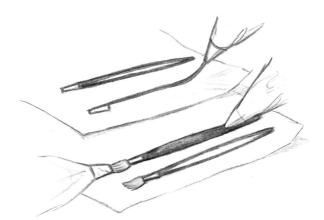

4 Colour half the remaining fondant icing (about 175g/6oz) blue. Roll out into lengths approximately 5cm (2inches) wide – or the height of the cake. Trim and wrap all the way round the cake. Smooth the top edge into the white icing evenly, smooth over the joins and trim off excess around the base.

5 Colour the remaining fondant in different shades of brown. Blend the pieces together roughly and roll out on a surface dusted with icing sugar or cornflour to give a marbled brown effect. Cut out four long strips and use to cover the cake drum around the cake, securing on with a little royal icing and trimming to fit.

6 Form a little cone of non-stick paper, colour a small amount of royal icing black and place in the cone. Snip the very tip to form a small nozzle. Use this to ice an outline on to waxed paper of two 20cm (8inch) paint brushes. Then pipe inside the outlines to fill. Colour a little more royal icing brown, put in a piping bag and pipe a little on the tips to give the brush ends. Leave to dry thoroughly for 24 hours.

7 Meanwhile, divide the remaining royal icing into eight and colour each one in different colours of your choice to form the paint blocks. Fill the eight indentations on the paintbox, and put a few 'pools' on to the paintbox lid. Also place a small portion of mixed icing on to the tips of the paint brushes.

8 To make the fondant cloth, take a small ball of spare fondant, place it on a piece of non-stick paper and roll out very thinly. Trim the fondant, *with* the paper underneath, to a square. Press a sieve gently over the surface to create a textured effect. Then, bend and scrunch the paper with the fondant to form a folded cloth appearance. Place on the cake drum next to the paintbox. The paper should be left underneath until eating to support the creased fondant cloth.

9 The next day, paint the 'metal ends' on the brushes with silver food colouring. When dry, carefully peel the brushes off the paper and secure on to the lid with a little spare royal icing. If liked, extra artist's paint tubes can be made out of leftover fondant, and painted silver once dry. Add a little coloured royal icing oozing out of the tube mouths for extra authenticity. Finally, wrap the ribbon around the edge of the cake drum, securing with glue or a little royal icing.

Magic Fairy Castle

*T*his fairy castle in the clouds has been asleep for a hundred years and the briars are beginning to take over. Lustre powder has been used to great effect here, giving a lovely ephemeral glimmer to the castle. Set aside a little time to make this cake, as it is quite time-consuming.

Ingredients

20×25×7.5cm (8×10×3inch) deep rectangular Victoria sponge cake (p.9)

18cm (7inch) deep round Victoria sponge cake (p.9)

900g (2lb) fondant icing (p.13)

apricot glaze (p.15)

675g (1½lb) marzipan (p.14)

4 ice-cream cones

100g (4oz) royal icing (p.13)

lustre powder (optional)

food colourings: purple, black, blue, brown, green

icing sugar or cornflour for dusting

Materials and decoration

25cm (10inch) round cake drum

length of purple ribbon (optional)

Equipment

5cm (2inch) plain round cutter

5.5cm (2¼inch) plain round cutter

tiny round plain cutter or bottle cap

paint brush

piping bag with fine writing (No.1) nozzle

Method

1 Take about 100g (4oz) of the fondant and colour it a light shade of purple. Roll out to a large circle on a surface dusted with icing sugar or cornflour and use to cover the top of the cake drum. If using, wrap the ribbon around the edge of the drum and secure with a little icing.

2 Using the 5cm (2inch) cutter, cut out six circles from the rectangular cake. With the 5.5cm (2¼inch) cutter, cut out six more circles.

3 Level the top of the round cake and place on the cake drum. Brush with some of the apricot glaze. Roll out half the marzipan (about 350g/12oz) to a large circle on a surface dusted with icing sugar or cornflour and use to cover the round cake.

4 Brush the tops of all the little circles of cake with glaze. Place three of the wider ones on top of each other to form the first tower. Place two of the thinner ones on top of each other to form the second tower. Slice another wide round in two horizontally and place one half on top of the two remaining wide rounds to form the third tower. Then, cut one thin round in two horizontally and place one half on top of the three remaining thin rounds to form the fourth and last tower (see illustration).

5 Roll out the remaining marzipan to wrap around each tower. Brush the marzipan with apricot glaze, place a tower on one end and roll up, joining the seam neatly. Repeat for all the towers.

6 Divide the remaining fondant into four piles. Take one pile and colour four different shades of purple (use the food colouring in gradually increasing quantities). Roll out in the same way as the marzipan and use to cover all four towers. Place the towers close together on top of the base cake.

7 Colour two more piles of fondant in different shades of grey (using a tiny amount of black food colouring). Mould with your fingers into small boulders and rocks. Press these around the sides of the cake and up around the base of the towers.

8 Using the back of a knife, score a brick pattern into the sides of the towers and make indentations for the cross-shaped windows.

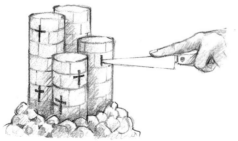

9 Colour the remaining fondant in different shades of blue, and, with a tiny round cutter or bottle cap, cut out lots of circles. Cut these in half to form the tiles for the roofs of the towers. Use the trimmings to form four cone-shaped tips for the turrets.

10 Place an upturned ice-cream cone on top of each tower and, starting at the bottom, tile each roof with the half-circles, using royal icing for cement and overlapping each row and mixing the shades. Press the cone tips on top of the towers.

11 Using a brush dipped lightly in purple food colouring (mixed with a little water for lighter shades), colour the windows dark purple and tint the bricks all over the towers different shades of lavender.

12 Colour some royal icing dark brown, and using a piping bag with a fine writing nozzle, pipe wiggly lines of briar creeping from the base of the castle and winding up the sides of some of the towers. Colour the remaining royal icing green and pipe leaves on to the briar.

13 Finally, brush the roofs with lustre powder if desired to give a 'magical' sparkly effect.

Pixie's Toadstool

What can be behind this shy pixie's door? For a lovely surprise when cutting into this toadstool cake, you could hollow out the cake before covering it with icing, and fill it with little sweets – 'a crock of gold at the end of the rainbow'!

Ingredients

12cm (5inch) deep round Victoria sponge cake (p.9)
1.85ltr (3¼pt) mixing bowl Victoria sponge cake (p.9)
apricot glaze (p.15)
450g (1lb) marzipan (p.14)
900g (2lb) fondant icing (p.13)
100g (4oz) royal icing (p.13)
liquorice allsorts
100g (4oz) desiccated coconut
extra marzipan for caterpillars or more pixies (optional)
food colourings: red, brown, pink, green, black
icing sugar or cornflour for dusting

Materials and decoration

30cm (12inch) round cake drum
length of green ribbon

Equipment

plain round cutters, of various sizes
paint brush
non-stick paper

Note: *Allow an extra day or overnight preparation time for icing to set.*

Method

1 Brush the sides of the round cake with apricot glaze. Roll out half the marzipan on a surface dusted with icing sugar or cornflour to a circle for covering the cake, and press on, smoothing over and trimming away excess around the base. Roll out and cover in turn with half the fondant. Keep all trimmings tightly wrapped until used to prevent drying out.

2 Trim the wide base of the mixing bowl cake so that it is level and turn it upside down. Carefully cut a thin wedge out of the cake. Brush the whole cake with apricot glaze, then roll out the remaining marzipan to a large circle to cover. Smooth the marzipan over the cake, including the underside and neatly going into the empty cut.

3 Colour three-quarters of the remaining fondant (about 350g/12oz) red and roll out to a circle as before. Use to cover the top rounded side of the mixing bowl cake, leaving the cut free and tucking the edges underneath.

4 Place the round cake in the centre of the cake drum (this is the toadstool 'stalk'). Place the red cake (the toadstool) on top of the stalk, securing with a little royal icing or water.

5 Roll out a little white fondant and, with different sized cutters, cut out various sizes of circle for the spots on the toadstool. Stick them with a dampened paint brush all over the top of the cake.

6 Colour a little piece of fondant brown and roll out to a small strip. Cut out an arched door, and a curved doorway arch that fits around it. Score wood panelling on to the door with the back of a knife and leave both the door and the archway to dry on non-stick paper overnight.

7 Meanwhile, use the marzipan trimmings to model the pixie. Divide the marzipan into portions and colour them pale pink and green. Use the pink marzipan to mould a pixie's head, and add pink pointed ears and a green

cap. Shape a green arm with a pink hand which will bend around the door, and a green pointed foot. Leave the pixie to dry on non-stick paper.

8 The next day, paint the shape of the door on the stalk with black food colouring. Carefully paint eyes, a nose, a mouth and rosy cheeks on to the pixie's face. Paint brown wood markings and black knots on to the brown door, and paint light brown 'mushroom' markings into the white wedge of the toadstool.

9 Stick the archway on to the toadstool stalk with a little royal icing. Secure the door to the archway so that it is ajar, and stick the pixie's head behind so that it is peeping out from behind the door. Place the foot at the base of the door, and attach the arm so that it looks as if it is holding the door open slightly.

10 Make a chimney with the liquorice allsorts and secure on to the toadstool roof. Colour the desiccated coconut with a little green food colouring and scatter on the cake drum around the toadstool, securing on to a thin layer of royal icing if preferred. Wrap green ribbon around the edge of the drum and secure.

11 Other pixies can be made in the same way as the first, if liked – or perhaps you might like to add some yellow-eyed green caterpillars to sit on top of the toadstool. Spare marzipan trimmings can be used to make little flowers to surround the toadstool.

Children on a Roundabout

This is quite a simple cake to make as it is based on plain round sandwich cakes. It is very appealing however, and if you do have a turntable it would be a lovely idea to present the roundabout cake on it for a spinning effect.
If you prefer, white almond paste could be used instead of the fondant – it is just as pliable, but does give a harder finish and added flavour. The children on the roundabout can be made as intricate as your time or patience allows – the effect of the girl's plaits streaming in the wind is quite easy to achieve.

Ingredients

three 20cm (8inch) round sandwich cherry and almond-flavoured Victoria sponge cakes (p.9)

900g (2lb) marzipan (p.14)

225g (8oz) orange buttercream (p.15)

food colourings: red, green, pink, blue, yellow, black, brown

icing sugar or cornflour for dusting

Materials and decoration

25cm (10inch) round cake drum

6 long 'bendy' straws

cocktail stick (optional)

length of red ribbon

Equipment

non-stick paper

piping bag with fine writing (No.1) nozzle

pastry wheel

paint brush

Note: *Allow an extra day or overnight preparation time for icing to set.*

Method

1   Colour 225g (8oz) of the marzipan (about a quarter) with red food colouring and roll out thinly on a surface dusted with icing sugar or cornflour. Cut out a 23cm (9inch) circle and leave to harden on non-stick paper for at least 24 hours. Keep the marzipan trimmings, tightly wrapped, for later.

2   Place 30ml (2tbsp) of the buttercream in a piping bag fitted with a fine writing nozzle and reserve.

3   Place one sandwich cake on the cake drum and cover the top and sides with some of the buttercream. Colour another 225g (8oz) of the marzipan green, and roll out into a long wide strip. Use to cover the top of the cake drum around the sandwich cake, taking it up the sides of the cake as well. Smooth into the corners and trim away excess from around the top and base.

4   Place the red marzipan circle on top of the cake on the drum – it will overlap the cake slightly. Spread a little buttercream over the centre of the marzipan circle and place the second cake on top of this. Spread over with more buttercream, add the remaining cake, then cover the top and sides of the entire cake area with the remaining buttercream.

5   Colour another 225g (8oz) of marzipan with pink food colouring. Roll out half of this to a 20cm (8inch) round to fit the top of the cake. Press on and trim around the edges. Using a pastry wheel (either a smooth-edged one or with an uneven edge for a wiggly line), make a spiral decoration on the circle and position it on the cake.

6 Roll out the remaining pink marzipan to a long strip. Mark on parallel lines with the pastry wheel and then use it to wrap round the sides of the cake. (You may find this easier to do in two sections.)

7 Make six small balls out of the red marzipan trimmings, each about the size of a pea, and press them gently into the red base, spacing evenly apart. Press the mouth end of the bendy straws into each ball to secure. Bend the straws over the top of the cake and then trim their ends so that the points meet in the centre of the cake. Secure these in place in the centre with a large ball of pink marzipan.

8 Now make the children: roll out a thick sausage of marzipan about 9cm (3½inches) long. Flatten slightly and slice with a knife to cut out separate limbs. Using your fingers, smooth and shape the limbs so that they look more realistic. Roll balls of paste for the heads and position on top of larger balls for the bodies. Secure the bodies to the cake with a little water, bending the limbs as necessary to give a suitable posture. Make about three children in all.

9 Colour little pieces of marzipan in appropriate shades for the children's clothing: perhaps green, blue and yellow. Tuck the clothes around the bodies – they can be as simple or as detailed as you like. Using a brush, paint the facial features with black and brown or red colouring. A ball can be made if liked by rolling a ball of spare marzipan and painting on wedges of colour.

10 To pipe hair, use the reserved buttercream in the piping bag. (Sifting a little cocoa powder over will give an effective browny-yellow tinge to the hair, if liked.) For a girl with plaits, push two pieces of a cocktail stick into the back of her head and pipe over these. Finally, wrap the ribbon around the edge of the cake drum and secure on with glue or royal icing.

Stable of Ponies

*M*any little girls have a period of 'pony mania' and this cake should definitely appeal. If you are making the cake for someone with a pony or with a favourite horse character in a book, make the ponies in the stable in their appropriate colours, and pipe the names over the doors. The bundles of hay and jumps add a touch of fun – they are made, respectively, out of shredded wheat and a stripey straw with an icing ladder.

Ingredients

two 24×30cm (9½×12inch) rectangular madeira cakes (p.12)

350g (12oz) buttercream (p.15)

apricot glaze (p.15)

900g (2lb) fondant icing (p.13)

450g (1lb) royal icing (p.13)

food colourings: yellow, brown, black, red, pink, green

icing sugar or cornflour for dusting

Materials and decoration

30cm (12inch) square cake drum

shredded wheat (optional)

1 striped straw (optional)

length of yellow ribbon

Equipment

non-stick paper

paint brush

piping bag with fine writing (No.1) nozzle and medium writing (No.2) nozzle

palette knife

Note: *Allow an extra day or overnight preparation time for icing to set.*

Method

1 Divide each rectangular cake in half widthways and sandwich one on top of the other with buttercream to give a four-storey cake. Cut a sloping roof each side, coming down nearly half-way.

2 Carve two holes into one long side of the cake to form the upper halves of the doorways. These holes should be about 5cm (2inches) square in area and 2.5cm (1inch) deep. Brush the insides of these holes with some apricot glaze.

3 Roll out a little white fondant (about 50g/2oz) on a surface dusted with icing sugar or cornflour. Cut out two squares (about 10cm/4inches) to line the holes. Press in and smooth, and trim the edges neatly. Secure the cake on to the cake drum with a little royal icing, and brush all over with glaze.

4 Colour half the remaining fondant yellow (keep unused fondant tightly wrapped to prevent drying), with a little brown added if required to give the appropriate wall shade. Roll out to 5mm (¼inch) thickness.

5 Measure the height and width of each of the sides of the cake (including the two short ends), and cut out pieces of non-stick paper to the same dimensions. Place these over the yellow icing and cut out a front side, a back side, and the two ends. Cover the cake with the appropriate pieces of fondant – for the front side with the holes, gently press on before neatly cutting around the holes and removing the pieces of surplus fondant. Smooth over the joins of 'window' and 'wall'.

6 Measure the height and width of the two roof sides and cut out pieces of non-stick paper in the same way. Colour three-quarters of the remaining fondant, about 300g (10oz), with black or dark brown food colouring. Roll out half to a large square, place the roof-sized pieces of paper over and use to cut out the icing. Cover the two sides of the roof. Roll out the remaining black/brown icing to the same dimensions on non-stick paper, trim to shape and slice into evenly-shaped squares with a knife for the tiles. Leave to dry for 24 hours. Also, cut out two little black name plaques from trimmings to go above the doors, and leave to dry. (Keep all the remaining black trimmings tightly wrapped for later use.)

7 Meanwhile, for the stable doors, colour some fondant yellowy-brown. Roll out and cut out four 5cm (2inch) squares. Lightly score each vertically for wood panelling. Using yellow-brown trimmings, cut out three thin strips for the straps on each of the four doors, and position diagonally across each door, securing on with a dampened paint brush. Leave the doors to dry on non-stick paper.

8 Colour half the remaining fondant grey with a tiny amount of black food colouring and model a horse's head. Use the remaining fondant (with trimmings as necessary) to form a second, brown, horse's head. Leave both to dry on non-stick paper. At the same time, colour two pieces of fondant trimmings red and yellow, and model into small rosettes to go above the stable doors. Leave to harden on non-stick paper.

9 The next day, place the black fondant tiles all over the roof, in neat overlapping rows, securing them on with a little water or royal icing. Press on firmly. Roll out the reserved black fondant trimmings and cut out a strip the length of the roof and about 2.5cm (1inch) wide. Place this on the very top of the roof so that it bends over on each side.

10 Fix the stable doors on to the wall with royal icing, with the upper doors opening outwards. Place the horses inside the stable holes, securing them with royal icing and positioning them so that their heads peep out over the doors. Stick the black plaques above the doorways, and the rosettes on each side.

11 Place a little royal icing in a piping bag with a fine writing nozzle. Pipe the names of the horses on to the plaques. Colour a little more royal icing pink, keep tightly wrapped, and colour the remaining royal icing green. Place a little of this in a piping bag with a medium writing nozzle, and pipe a green branching tree on to one end of the stable. Place the pink icing in the piping bag and use to pipe blossom all over the tree.

12 Spread all the remaining green royal icing over the cake drum around the stable, and stipple it to create a grass effect by placing the flat side of a palette knife on to the icing and drawing it upwards in little strokes. Add shredded wheat bundles of hay tied with black thread and a little jump made from halved straws and brown icing ladders, if liked. Finally, wrap the ribbon around the edge of the cake drum, securing on with a little glue or royal icing.

Space Rocket over Planet Earth

This exciting cake on a popular theme is very easy to make. The special tube shapes for the rocket are achieved by baking cake mixture in empty food cans – just make up the required raw cake quantity as shown in the chart on page 12. The rocket can be decorated in the colours of the country of your choice. Silver food colouring is used to great effect here, but it is advisable not to eat too much, even though a non-toxic brand is used, as the taste is not very pleasant.

Ingredients

quantity for 20cm (8inch) square madeira cake (p.12)
175g (6oz) buttercream (p.15)
1.5kg (3lb) fondant icing (p.13)
225g (8oz) royal icing (p.13)
food colourings: blue, black, green, silver, red, orange
icing sugar or cornflour for dusting

Materials and decoration

40cm (16inch) square cake drum
length of blue ribbon (optional)

Equipment

two 850g (1lb14oz)) empty food cans, both ends removed
450g (1lb) empty food can, both ends removed
non-stick paper
baking tray
egg box
paint brush

Note: *Allow an extra day or overnight preparation time for icing to set.*

Method

1 Line the three cans with non-stick paper and place on a greased baking tray. Divide the cake mixture between them. Bake in a preheated 170°C (325°F/Gas Mark 3) oven for 1¼ hours for the large cans and 1 hour for the smaller. Turn out and cool thoroughly on a wire rack.

2 Trim the top surfaces of all the cakes and divide each horizontally into three. Sandwich all nine pieces together with buttercream, with the larger pieces at the bottom and the smaller pieces at the top. Trim the top large piece on one side so that it slopes to join with the first small piece, and trim the very top small piece in the same way. Cover the entire cake with the remaining buttercream.

3 Colour a third of the fondant (about 450g/1lb) dark blue and roll out to a large square. Cover the cake drum, securing with a little water. Trim away excess around the base.

4 Roll out a piece of white fondant and cut out a quarter circle to fit into one corner of the cake drum. Position this on the drum, fixing on with a little water. Leave to harden.

5 Roll out half the remaining fondant, about 450g (1lb), to a large rectangle on a surface dusted with icing sugar or cornflour. Wrap it around the cake, positioning the join underneath and smoothing the fondant into the corners so that the shape is clear. Trim away excess around the base. Secure the rocket to the cake drum with royal icing.

6 Mould the hollow rocket boosters by pushing pieces of fondant into egg boxes dusted with cornflour. Trim the tops and leave to dry before turning out.

7 Colour another piece of fondant black, roll out and cut three strips about 2cm (¾inch) wide and long enough to wrap around the rocket. Fix around the rocket with royal icing: one at the base, one half way up the main part of the body, and one at the very top. Roll out a piece of white fondant to make three strips in the same way, and position these alongside the black strips. Cut another, larger (7.5cm/3inch wide), strip of white fondant, and attach around the neck of the rocket where it narrows. Leave to dry. At the same time, mould a large cone-shaped rocket module from white fondant and leave to dry on non-stick paper overnight.

8 Using a brush and diluted green and blue food colouring, paint the quarter globe of white on the cake drum so that it looks like Earth. Paint green areas to show land, allow to dry and then paint the white areas blue for the sea.

9 Paint black and silver squares on to the large strip of white fondant surrounding the neck of the rocket to give a chequered design. Then, using silver food colouring, paint the rocket boosters, the rocket module, and the white strips alongside the black. Paint silver stars on to the dark blue board.

10 Fix the rocket module to the tip of the rocket with royal icing, and the rocket boosters around the base. Cut a thin strip of white fondant, score with light lines and attach around the module.

11 Colour a little remaining fondant red, and cut out and press on a numeral for the rocket. Cut out a rectangle of white fondant for a flag, secure on and paint in appropriate colours – perhaps black or blue and red for an American flag. Other planets can be made out of discs of spare fondant if liked; place on the drum among the stars and paint appropriately – perhaps orange. If liked, wrap the ribbon around the edge of the cake drum, securing on with a little royal icing.

Pirate's Treasure Chest

Any budding Blackbeard or Captain Hook would be thrilled to find this buried chest of treasure, filled to the brim with stolen loot. Perhaps you could hold a treasure hunt during the party, with the cake as the prize at the end of the trail.

Ingredients

25cm (10inch) deep round Victoria sponge cake (p.9)

apricot glaze (p.15)

350g (12oz) marzipan (p.14)

675g (1½lb) fondant icing (p.13)

100g (4oz) royal icing (p.13)

chocolate coins, sweetie 'jewels', rings, bracelets and gold bars

food colourings: brown, black, yellow, plus other colours of choice

icing sugar or cornflour for dusting

Materials and decoration

2 wooden skewers or thin dowells

32.5cm (13inch) round cake drum

large sheet of medium sandpaper

glue

chopstick

length of yellow ribbon

Equipment

non-stick paper

paint brush

Note: *Allow an extra day or overnight preparation time for icing to set.*

Method

1 Cut out a 10×20cm (4×8inch) rectangle from the centre of the cake, and carefully cut out three half-moon shapes from the spare sponge. (These half-moons will form the lid of the chest.)

2 Turn the rectangle upside down and carve out a hollow from the centre, leaving a frame of at least 1cm (½inch) and a depth of about half the cake. Brush all over the outside and inside with apricot glaze.

3 Lay the three semi-circles of cake alongside each other, rounded sides up. Holding firmly in one hand, trim to the same length as the long side of the rectangle. Secure the cakes together with a little apricot glaze and brush all over with the remaining glaze. Push two wooden skewers through all three cakes to secure, and trim the ends of the skewers on both sides.

4 Roll out two-thirds of the marzipan (about 225g/8oz) to a large rectangle on a surface dusted with icing sugar or cornflour and cover the rectangular cake, smoothing into the hollow and over the edges, and trimming away excess around the base. Roll out the remaining marzipan to a large thin circle and use to cover the entire semi-circular 'lid'. Smooth the corners and trim away any excess.

5 Colour two-thirds of the fondant (about 450g/1lb) dark brown. (Keep unused fondant tightly wrapped to prevent drying out.) Roll out into a large rectangle and a large circle (both the same size as the marzipan pieces) and use to cover both the base chest and the lid. Smooth into the hollows and around the curves, and make sure that the corners are neat.

6 Colour about two-thirds of the remaining fondant – about 150g (5oz) – with black food colouring. Roll it out on a surface dusted with icing sugar or cornflour and cut out thin strips for the 'metal' edging on the chest. Stick these on to the base and lid with a little royal icing or water.

7 Also mould from black fondant a loop and a catch. Leave these to dry on non-stick paper. Cut out a small black rectangle to form the 'Jolly Roger' and, using a little white fondant, cut out a skull and crossbones and stick on with a little water. Wrap in cling film until needed to prevent the icing from drying out.

8 Cover the cake drum with the sandpaper, securing it on with glue and folding the edges under neatly. Place the cake base (the treasure chest) in the centre of the drum.

9 Mould some bones from a piece of white fondant and leave to dry on non-stick paper. Colour the remaining fondant a pale cream colour (use a tiny amount of diluted yellow food colouring) and knead in a tiny amount of brown until almost mixed in but still a bit 'muddy'. Roll out to a largish square, about 10×12.5cm (4×5inches) – this will be the map – and trim. (Use the trimmings to mould a starfish, if liked – and mark on a pattern with a fork.) Drape the map over the corner of the chest and make a few tears in it. Unwrap the Jolly Roger from its cling film and drape over the other corner of the chest. Leave to dry overnight.

10 The next day, attach all the lock fittings to the chest with royal icing and let dry. Using a brush and appropriate food colourings, paint signs on to the map – including 'X' marks the spot. Paint black knots and wood markings on to the chest and lid.

11 Insert a wooden chopstick into one corner of the lid and press it into the back corner of the chest as a support. Secure the lid along the back edge of the chest by using royal icing as a 'hinge'.

12 Fill the chest with the chocolate coins, jewels and other treasure, piling it up so as to hide the chopstick in the corner. Wrap the ribbon around the edge of the cake drum, securing with glue or a little royal icing.

Helter-Skelter

*T*his fun-filled cake needs patience and a steady hand, but is stunning when it is finished. The special cake shapes used to form the helter-skelter are obtained by part-filling pudding basins with raw cake mixture, resulting in shallow domed cakes. These are placed on top of a complete pudding basin cake made in the normal way.

Ingredients

quantity for 15cm (6inch) square madeira cake (p.12)

1.1ltr (2pint) pudding basin madeira cake (p.12)

350g (12oz) buttercream (p.15)

45ml (3tbsp) raspberry jam

225g (8oz) royal icing (p.13)

900g (2lb) fondant icing (p.13)

50g (2oz) desiccated coconut

food colourings: red, blue, silver, brown, yellow, and other colours of choice

icing sugar or cornflour for dusting

Materials and decoration

30cm (12inch) round cake drum

cocktail sticks

rice paper

length of blue ribbon

Equipment

250ml (½pint) ovenproof pudding basin

500ml (1pint) ovenproof pudding basin

string

fine sandpaper

piping bag with medium writing (No.2) nozzle

non-stick paper

paint brush

Method

1 Divide the raw cake mixture between the 250ml (½pint) and the 500ml (1pint) pudding basins and bake in a 170°C (325°F/Gas Mark 3) oven – 50 minutes for the small bowl and 1 hour for the large. Cool in the basins before turning out.

2 Place all three cakes on top of each other, with the largest at the base and the smallest on top. Holding firmly with one hand, trim slightly with a knife to a gently sloping cone shape. Still maintaining the shape, sandwich all the pieces of cake together with some of the buttercream and raspberry jam. Transfer to the cake drum wih care, securing on with a little royal icing. Cover the entire cake with the remaining buttercream.

Note: *Allow an extra day or overnight preparation time for icing to set.*

3 Colour a little over half the fondant – about 575g (1¼lb) – red. Roll out most of this (450g/1lb) to a large circle and use to cover the cake, smoothing down over the sides and over the join. Neatly trim the excess away from around the top and base. (Keep all the red trimmings, tightly wrapped.)

4 Keeping back a little fondant for the door and children (about 100g/4oz), colour the remaining fondant blue. (Keep all unused fondant tightly wrapped to prevent drying out.) Take half the blue fondant and form it into a cone shape that fits on top of the cake. Take the same amount of red fondant trimmings and form a similar-sized cone. Slice each cone into eight even wedges. Using four wedges of blue and four of red, reshape a new cone alternating the colours. Join the wedges together by dampening the surfaces and pressing together. Secure the cone to the top of the cake with a little royal icing.

5 Secure one end of string to the top of the body of the cake (not the tip of the cone), and wrap the string around and down the cake in a spiral. Secure it at the bottom, the angle becoming more gradual and eventually flat as it reaches the base.

6 Neatly cut cocktail sticks in halves and smooth the cut ends with sandpaper. Insert the cocktail sticks into the cake at 1cm (½inch) intervals along the line of the string, pushing in so that they stick out just over 1cm (½inch). Then, remove the string without disturbing the cocktail sticks and leave the cake to dry for 24 hours.

7 Cut a flag shape out of rice paper and paint a cocktail stick silver. Leave to dry. Once dried, moisten one end of the stick and secure the flag on to it. Make a second flag for the base of the helter-skelter in the same way, using chequered paper if liked.

8 Place some royal icing in a piping bag with a medium writing nozzle and pipe small trellised squares on to non-stick paper. (You will need enough trellises to equal the length of the string used to wind around the helter-skelter – about 40–50 in all.) Leave the trellises to dry. Meanwhile, pipe a row of decorative little white dots around the cone at the top of the cake.

9 Spread a little royal icing over the cake drum, colour the coconut brown and scatter it over the icing on the drum for fairground grass.

10 Once the cake has dried, roll out the reserved blue fondant (with any blue trimmings) into long strips, 5mm (¼inch) thick and 1cm (½inch) wide. Brush one edge of the strips with a dampened brush and carefully place them against the cake so that they are supported by the cocktail sticks. Neaten the joins of the strips as you go along, and press them gently into the side of the cake with your fingers. Secure the slide at the bottom and leave to dry. Paint the trellises with silver food colouring and allow to dry.

11 Meanwhile, tint a small amount of the reserved fondant yellow for the door. Roll out and cut out a small door shape, and secure on to the bottom of the helter-skelter with a little water. Make a little fondant handle, and attach on to the door. Next make the children to go on the slide – colour the reserved fondant in appropriate colours, model and keep to one side on non-stick paper. To make the mats, cut out little squares of brown fondant and then pipe some brown royal icing over in dots for the upper surfaces of the mats.

12 When the trellises are dry, secure them along the edge of the fondant slide using small amounts of royal icing. Then gently place the children into the helter-skelter, and make a pile of mats at the bottom. Place one flag in position at the top of the helter-skelter and another at the base to mark the pile of mats. Paint the door handle silver if liked. Finally, wrap the ribbon around the edge of the cake drum, securing with glue or a little royal icing.

Hot-air Balloons

The patterns on these elegant hot-air balloons can be as detailed as you wish – perhaps you might like to make fondant stripes, zig-zags or spots, or pipe on old-fashioned loops and tassels of rope.

Ingredients

2ltr (4pt) pudding basin madeira cake (p.12)

1.5kg (3lb) fondant icing (p.13)

175g (6oz) buttercream (p.15)

225g (8oz) marzipan (p.14)

225g (8oz) royal icing (p.13)

food colourings: yellow, blue, green, red, brown, silver

icing sugar or cornflour for dusting

Materials and decoration

38cm (15inch) square cake drum

length of pale blue ribbon (optional)

Equipment

non-stick paper

sieve

paint brush

piping bag with fine writing (No.1) nozzle and medium writing (No.2) nozzle

Note: *Allow an extra day or overnight preparation time for icing to set.*

Method

1 Roll out a third of the fondant (about 450g/1lb) on a surface dusted with icing sugar or cornflour and use to cover the cake drum, smoothing on and trimming away excess around the edges. Leave to dry.

2 Split the cake in half horizontally and sandwich together again with some of the buttercream. Coat the entire surface of the cake with the remaining buttercream.

3 Take half the marzipan and mould it into a cone shape to make the 'point' at the base of the balloon. Press on to the end of the cake. Mould the other half of marzipan into a shallow semi-circle and place on the top of the cake to make a more pronounced globe shape.

4 Take another third of fondant (about 450g/1lb) and roll it out on a surface dusted with icing sugar or cornflour to a 30cm (12inch) circle, large enough to cover the pudding basin cake. Cover the cake, tucking the fondant underneath and squaring the bottom end slightly over the marzipan cone.

5 Divide the remaining fondant into three portions, about 150g (5oz) each. Colour one portion creamy-yellow and one blue. Divide the third portion into three again, and colour one piece green, one red and one yellow.

6 Roll out the creamy-yellow fondant to a large strip that will wrap around the middle third of the balloon. Lay over the cake and press on. Similarly, roll out the blue fondant in the same way to cover the bottom third of the balloon, easing over the shaped area and trimming off. Then roll out the green, red and yellow pieces separately and cut out two large wedges or triangles of each, to fit the top third of the balloon. Lay the coloured triangles over the top third of the balloon, alternating the colours and trimming the edges neatly. (Keep the trimmings of all the coloured fondant, tightly wrapped in cling film, for making the small balloons later.)

7 With your fingers dusted with icing sugar or cornflour, mould the balloon into shape and pinch in four gentle ridges, spaced evenly apart and pointing downwards. Keep the balloon to one side on non-stick paper.

8 Gather up some fondant trimmings and colour them brown. Mould into a basket shape and place on non-stick paper. Press a sieve gently over the basket to give a textured effect.

9 Using spare trimmings of coloured fondant, mould the little decorative hot-air balloons and baskets in various designs. Also mould two little passengers for the large basket, and a tiny cone-shaped burner.

10 When the cake drum is dry and hard, paint the surface with diluted blue, green and yellow food colourings to give a subtle sky effect. To make the colours fade into each other, apply the paint and then while still wet make gentle brushstrokes across the area where the colours join. Leave to dry.

11 Place the large balloon on the sky, and position the basket a little way underneath it. Secure both to the drum with a little spare royal icing. Place the tiny balloons and their baskets on the drum around the sky. Attach the little burner to the base of the large balloon and insert the passengers into the large basket, fixing in with royal icing. You may also like to cut out a 'horizon' of white fondant and press on to the base of the cake drum to resemble hills below.

12 Place a little white royal icing into a piping bag with a fine writing nozzle and pipe decorative loops on to the large balloon where the different colours join, and on to the smaller balloons. Colour the remaining royal icing brown and pipe with a medium writing nozzle attachment ropes between the large basket and the balloon. If desired, a message could also be piped on to the middle band of the balloon. Use the smaller nozzle (No.1) to pipe the ropes on the smaller balloons.

13 Finally, paint the top attachment rope on the balloons with silver food colouring, and the little burner. Paint the horizon pale green with diluted colouring, and little black seagulls in the sky if liked. Wrap the ribbon around the edge of the cake drum, if using, securing on with a little royal icing.

Friendly Tortoise

Younger children will love this simple cake, especially if they have a pet tortoise of their own. The shell is covered with little tiles made out of fondant, first coloured in various shades of yellow, brown and orange. These tiles are then decorated with a painted pattern, but if you have time, more complicated swirls could be piped over with brown royal icing.
Perhaps the tortoise should be presented to the table in a shoebox on a bed of paper straw!

Ingredients

1.85ltr (3¼pint) mixing bowl Victoria sponge cake (p.9)
apricot glaze (p.15)
675g (1½lb) marzipan (p.14)
675g (1½lb) fondant icing (p.13)
100g (4oz) royal icing (p.13)
100g (4oz) desiccated coconut
food colourings: brown, yellow, orange, black, green
icing sugar or cornflour for dusting

Materials and decoration

35cm (14inch) round cake drum
length of green ribbon

Equipment

paint brush
piping bag with fine writing (No.1) nozzle

Method

1 Place the cake upside down on the centre of the cake drum. Brush all over with apricot glaze. Roll out the marzipan on a surface dusted with icing sugar or cornflour to a large circle and use to cover the cake, smoothing down over the sides and tucking the edges under the cake.

2 Colour a third of the fondant (about 225g/8oz) in different shades of brown, yellow and orange. Roll out on a surface dusted with icing sugar or cornflour and cut into evenly-sized tiles.

3 Fit the fondant tiles like a jigsaw over the back of the shell, using royal icing as cement. Try to make a balanced pattern of the different shades.

4 Colour another third of the fondant icing (about 225g/8oz) dark brown. Use to mould a tortoise's head (with eyelids), four feet, and a tail. Secure these to the cake at the appropriate ends with a little royal icing.

5 Colour the last third of fondant yellow and roll into a thick long sausage, the length of the circumference of the bottom of the cake. Flatten each end of the roll, but leave the centre rounded. Wrap around the base of the cake, joining the ends at the back of the tortoise. (The fatter part of the strip should be over the head.) Slightly raise the yellow strip where it goes over the feet and head.

6 Using a brush and a little brown food colouring, paint light swirls on to each tile for a decorative effect.

7 Make two tiny eyes out of icing and place on the head. Colour the remaining royal icing black and place in a piping bag. Pipe five claws on to each foot, and pipe beady eyes on to the head. Make a yellow and white flower out of fondant for the tortoise if liked, and perhaps a couple of green fondant lettuce leaves.

8 Finally, colour the desiccated coconut green and scatter over the cake drum. Wrap the ribbon around the edge of the drum, securing on with a little glue or royal icing.

LIST OF SUPPLIERS

Although the recipes for making icing and marzipan used in this book are quite simple and quick, you may prefer to buy these ingredients ready-made or ready-to-mix, to save time and effort. There are many good quality products on the market, available from most branches of superior supermarkets, grocers and specialist kitchen and baking stores. A few are listed below, and also a list of mail-order suppliers for all the products you may need – equipment, fondant icing, royal icing, marzipan, and food colourings.

Fondant icing can be obtained ready-made from many supermarkets, for instance, to name just two brands, Sainsbury's, Whitworths and Renshaws market 225g (8oz) packets. Many mail-order and retail specialists make their own icing too. Royal icing is now sold in 500g packets from Whitworths and Silver Spoon among others, and just needs the addition of water. There are many brands of marzipan available – choose a softer, flexible variety if possible. One thing to remember generally is that bought icings do take a little longer to dry hard than home-made, so take this into account when planning your timetable.

Retail outlets

Kitchens
167 Whiteladies Road, Bristol,
Avon, BS8 2SQ
Tel: 0272 739614
and 4–5 Quiet Street, Bath,
Avon, BA1 2JS
Tel: 0225 330524

Retail and mail-order

Covent Garden Kitchen Supplies
North Row, The Market, Covent Garden,
London, WC2 8RA
Tel: 01 836 9167

David Mellor
4 Sloane Square, London, SW1W 8EE
Tel: 01 730 4259
and 26 James Street, Covent Garden,
London, WC2E 8PA
Tel: 01 379 6947
and 66 King Street,
Manchester, M2 4NP
Tel: 061 834 7023

Divertimenti
68–72 Marylebone Lane,
London, W1H 5FF
Tel: 01 935 0689
and 139–141 Fulham Road,
London, SW3 6SD
Tel: 01 581 8065

Elizabeth David Ltd.
46 Bourne Street, London, SW1W 8JD
Tel: 01 730 3123

Homebakers Supplies
157–159 High Street, Wolstanton,
Newcastle, Staffs, ST5 0EJ
Tel: 0782 614119

Jenny Campbell Trading/B.R. Mathews & Son
12 Gypsy Hill, Upper Norwood,
London, SE19 1NN
Tel: 01 670 0788

Mary Ford Cake Artistry Centre Ltd.
28–30 Southbourne Grove, Southbourne,
Bournemouth, Dorset, BH6 3RA
Tel: 0202 431001/422653

Squires Kitchen
The Potteries, Pottery Lane,
Wrecclesham, Farnham, Surrey, GU10 4QJ
Tel: 0252 711749

Woodnutt's Ltd.
97 Church Road, Hove, Sussex, BN3 2BA
Tel: 0273 205353

Mail-order

Cookcraft Club Ltd.
20 Canterbury Road, Herne Bay,
Kent, CT6 5DJ

Craft Centres
360 Leach Place, Bamber Bridge,
Preston, Lancashire, PR5 8AR
Tel: 0772 34848

Guy Paul & Co. Ltd.
Unit 84, A1 Industrial Park,
Little End Road, Eaton Socon,
Cambridgeshire, PE19 3JH
Tel: 0480 72545

INDEX

ACKNOWLEDGEMENTS

Maxine Clark made the cakes on
pages 32, 39, 48, 63, 82, 85, 91, 94,
106 and 115. **Joanna Farrow** made
the cakes on pages 26, 35, 45, 54,
60, 66, 70, 73, 76, 97. **Kathy Man**
made the cakes on pages 29, 42,
51, 57, 79, 88, 100, 103, 109, 112.